24224

Albuquerque Academy

D0016012

ham radio

AN INTRODUCTION TO

the world beyond

cb

Here is your passport to the fascinating world of amateur radio. Starting with a tour of an established radio station, authors Richard and Louis Kuslan explain all the procedures necessary for getting started in amateur radio—from qualifying tests through building and operating a "ham shack."

Pointers are given on how to choose transmitting and receiving equipment, and how to choose and build an antenna. Full descriptions of the correct operating procedures and helpful hints on where to get expert advice are also included.

RICHARD DAVID KUSLAN, WA1UAW
LOUIS I. KUSLAN, K1LK

ham radio
AN INTRODUCTION TO
the world beyond
cb

PRENTICE-HALL INC. Englewood Cliffs, N.J. 07632

Text Copyright ©1981 by Louis I. Kuslan and Richard D. Kuslan
Illustrations Copyright ©1981 by Prentice-Hall, Inc.
Interior design by Dawn L. Stanley

All rights reserved. No part of this book may be
reproduced in any form or by any means, except for
the inclusion of brief quotations in a review,
without permission in writing from the publisher.

Printed in the United States of America •J

PRENTICE-HALL INTERNATIONAL, INC., London
PRENTICE-HALL of AUSTRALIA, Pty. Ltd., North Sydney
PRENTICE-HALL of CANADA, LTD., Toronto
PRENTICE-HALL of INDIA PRIVATE LTD., New Delhi
PRENTICE-HALL of JAPAN, INC., Tokyo
PRENTICE-HALL of SOUTHEAST ASIA PTE. LTD., Singapore
WHITEHALL BOOKS LIMITED, Wellington, New Zealand

1 2 3 4 5 6 7 8 9 10

Library of Congress Cataloging in Publication Data
Kuslan, Richard.
  Ham radio.

   Bibliography: p.
   Includes index.
   SUMMARY: Discusses setting up and operating a ham
radio station, including obtaining the necessary equipment
and operator's license.
   1. Amateur radio stations--Juvenile literature.
 1. Amateur radio stations   I. Kuslan, Louis I.,
joint author.   II. Title.
TK9956.K86   621.3841'66   80-18327
ISBN 0-13-372334-8

To the hams of the world
for their unselfish public service.

Albuquerque Academy

24224

contents

ix

preface

Ham Radio was written to introduce boys and girls to a hobby which is enjoyed by more than a million people all over the world. This hobby is amateur, or, as it is popularly known, "ham," radio. Like anything worth doing, becoming a radio amateur takes some time and effort. You must take and pass a special government license test in order to become a ham. No test of any kind is required to operate a CB set, but you may not run an amateur transmitter on your own unless you have passed the license test. Unlike CB radio, however, the opportunities and rewards of ham radio are limitless. For this reason, CB'ers often turn away from CB operation in a few years and join the ranks of the amateurs.

Many young hams enter technical careers in the electronics industry because of the interest and skills developed as hams. Many others, probably the majority, are more excited by the opportunity to communicate with boys, girls, women and men on every continent. If you have had fun talking on your CB set with other CB'ers a few blocks or miles away, think of the thrill of speaking directly to hams in England, the Soviet Union, Japan and Australia with your own ham transmitter. Whatever your interest, there is something in amateur radio for everyone.

The writers of this book have been hams for eight years. They entered world of "ham radio" when Rich, then 12, returned from school where he had just entered the 7th grade, to tell his father that he would like to join the school ham radio club. Lou had experimented with radio as a boy, but had not become a ham. He was so pleased that he told Rich that he too would like to become a ham. Rich soon passed his Novice test and was licensed as WN1UAW, a call which soon become WA1UAW. Lou was licensed as WA1UB1 and a few years later as K1LK.

We enjoy this hobby so much that we decided to write a book in order to tell boys and girls about ham radio, and to draw their attention to a hobby which has grown by leaps and bounds. We hope to interest you in amateur radio by describing the fascinating things amateurs do, and then setting forth the steps to take to become an amateur. For this reason, our book is not intended to be a complete textbook on how to become a licensed amateur. Once you decide to become a ham, you will find more than enough help from the information sources listed and from local hams who will be happy to help you.

Chapter I, "The World of Amateur Radio," tells how Tom Sachs, a junior-high school boy, discovers ham radio and is introduced to a local amateur who becomes his guide. In Chapter II, "An Amateur Radio Station in Operation," Tom visits this new friend's shack and experiences the thrills of long distance communication between hams. Chapter III, "Getting Your License," focuses on the government test which Tom must take, and explains some of the things a Novice is expected to know in order to operate his or her first radio station. "Going on the Air," Chapter IV, describes the basic elements of a radio station such as the receiver, transmitter, antenna and key. Chapter V, "Hunting DX," introduces you to the excitement and the many achievement awards open to hams who make a specialty of hunting "DX" or foreign ham stations, particularly those from great distances and from regions where there are few radio amateurs. Since hams must know how to run their stations, Chapter VI, "Good Operating Procedure," explains the proper way of going on the air without interfering with other hams, and of operating efficiently and courteously.

Because Ham Radio is primarily written to interest you in amateur radio, it is non-technical. Therefore, as we have said, you will need to go to other sources for much of the information on which you will be tested. Chapter VI, "Where to Get Help," lists some of the books and magazine articles which may be helpful as you prepare. All are written for beginners.

As you read this book, you will meet many special words and abbreviations which hams use. These terms are explained the first time they appear. The Appendix at the back of the book will be handy for checking word meanings.

We hope that you will enjoy this book, and that it will guide you into a satisfying and enjoyable lifetime hobby. Many thousands of young people discover ham radio every year. We would be delighted to have you join their number. Perhaps Rich, WA1UAW or Lou, K1LK, will have the pleasure of talking to you in the near future on one of the ham bands. We look forward to a "FB QSO" with you.

"73"
Rich, WA1UAW
Lou, K1LK

1 the world of amateur radio

Tom Sachs ignores most radio commercials, but there is one commercial which is his favorite because it is the one that opened his eyes to the world of ham (amateur) radio. As he remembers it, he was watching a cartoon program one Saturday morning when Dick Van Dyke, a Hollywood star whom Tom has always liked, appeared on the TV screen and said, looking right at Tom:

> *Hi. Some of my friends are Amateur Radio Operators and they make friends for all of us with other hams all around the world. But more importantly, they stand ready with emergency communications any time we need them. And you see, Ham Radio is also a great training ground for the technical talent our country will need in the future. And any one, any age is welcome. Join in. Get free information from the American Radio Relay League, Newington, Connecticut, 06111.*

1

Tom was caught up by what Dick Van Dyke said because it brought to mind a newspaper story about three local hams who had "provided communications assistance" to searchers who were looking for a child lost in dense woods. In this story, the three hams ("What a crazy name that is," Tom thought) had talked about the help hams gave during such emergencies as automobile accidents, floods, and storms. But they had added—and this is what really intrigued Tom—the information that they spent much more of their spare time talking to fellow hams in such distant parts of the world as Europe, India, South Africa and Australia. The reporter quoted them as saying that anyone, including people with such severe handicaps as blindness or wheelchair confinement, could become hams with some study and effort.

The newspaper story referred to a number of radio amateurs who were celebrities. King Hussein of Jordan, Senator Barry Goldwater of Arizona, Joe Rudi of the Oakland Athletics, Stan Brokaw, TV news reporter and Jean Shepherd, radio humorist and writer, fit this classification, but most hams, it said, were "ordinary people like you and me." There were no social or occupational requirements in order to enter this hobby. One needed only a sincere desire to learn about radio and to communicate with similarly-minded girls and boys, women and men.

Dick Van Dyke brought all this back to Tom as the commercial ended with the words "Anyone, any age, is welcome. Join in."

If you are one of the millions of Americans who have seen this commercial or one of the other radio and TV commercials provided as a non-profit service by the American Radio Relay League (ARRL) and the broadcasting industry, you may well have said to yourself just as

Tom did, "I'd really like to know more about ham radio. I'll bet I could get a license and talk to other hams around the world."

No matter how or when you become interested, if you have not acted on this interest before, write to the Amateur Radio Relay League, Newington, Connecticut, 06111 for its free information package for beginners. Take advantage of this service from the ARRL, the voice of American hams, one of whose most important activities is that of helping newcomers to ham radio to become licensed radio operators. The ARRL was started in 1914 by Hiram Percy Maxim, a great American inventor, who had received one of the very first radio amateur licenses, 1AW. 1AW is now the internationally recognized call of the ARRL, but in the slightly changed form of W1AW. The ARRL, a non-profit organization with members in all states and U.S. territories, as well as in many foreign countries, has a membership of more than 150,000 active hams.

We expect that you will have many unanswered questions after reading this book and the ARRL special beginner's materials. Don't hesitate to write or to telephone the ARRL for help since their staff is ready and prepared to help. The most important communication you will receive from the ARRL is probably the name and address of the nearest amateur radio club or the name, address and call letters of a local ham who will be glad to have the opportunity to help you. The letter to Tom Sachs from the ARRL which gave him this information read:

Mr. Tom Sachs
235 Carolyn Street
Belleville, NH 03000

Dear Friend:

Thank you for contacting the American Radio Relay League about assistance in your efforts to increase your skills in amateur radio. Below is the name and address of someone involved in amateur radio instruction in your area. You are invited to contact this person for information about local classes or additional help. Good luck in your efforts to upgrade your skills in amateur radio and please let us know if we can provide further assistance.

Club and Training Department

For additional local assistance, please contact:
Mrs. Louise Grant, K1XXP
14 Tharp Avenue
Belleville, NH 03000   Telephone: 881-5372

W1AW, the ARRL headquarters call letters, and K1XXP, Louise Grant's call letters, mentioned above, are typical amateur calls. That is, they are a combination of letters and numbers assigned by the Federal Communications Commission as a special identification when the new ham is licensed. The call letters of the writers of this book are WA1UAW (Rich) and K1LK (Lou).

The ham who gives you that first round of encouraging help and who is ready and waiting whenever you call is, by tradition, called your 'Elmer," a name which is supposed to have been the first name of an old-timer in ham radio who introduced many boys and girls to the hobby. The sooner you call your "Elmer," the sooner you will be on your way to a call and a licensed radio station of your own.

Many beginners, however, prefer to take advantage of the help which their local amateur club, if there is one, will give freely. There is obviously a difference between the kind of assistance which an "Elmer" gives and that which a club can give. The "Elmer" provides a one-to-one personal relationship. He or she is usually available during the week for calls and visits. The "Elmer" is a guide and tutor, sometimes working very closely with the beginner; at other times, depending upon the learner's rate of progress, on hand at less frequent intervals. The radio amateur club, on the other hand, generally organizes a series of more or less formal classes for a group of beginners, as well as for already licensed amateurs who are studying for more advanced licenses. These classes, taught by volunteers, meet once a week for two or three hours in the evening for as long as necessary, usually for ten to fifteen weeks, ending when all their students who have stuck it out have taken and passed their Novice tests.

Thousands of amateurs owe their skill as hams to these volunteer teachers. Many people learn better in organized classes, whereas others prefer to work by themselves or with an "Elmer." Indeed, many hams have done it *all* by themselves, but they are usually people who have already gained experience with electronics and are not truly beginners in the field. You may be fortunate enough to be able to choose to work individually with one ham or to attend organized classes, or even to move ahead by yourself. Many hams have chosen to take advantage of both kinds of help, clubs and an "Elmer," and why not, if both are available?

Since Tom Sachs lived too far away from the nearest ham club to turn to it for help, he called his assigned "Elmer," Louise Grant, K1XXP as soon as he received his information letter from the ARRL. Although he had been somewhat surprised that his "Elmer's" name was Louise, he was happy that she lived near him. He had been surprised at first since he had never thought about the possibility of female hams. He soon discovered that there were some twenty thousand in the United States alone, and thousands more around the world. Tom was amused to learn that ham talk for female amateurs was YL ("young lady," if unmarried) and XYL ("ex-young" lady, if married). This seemed to be rather impolite even though it was balanced by the fact that male hams are often referred to as OM ("old man") whether young *or* old.

Louise, who was at home, greeted him cordially on the telephone, and invited Tom to visit her station that evening and to bring his parents. During their phone conversation, Louise asked Tom if he had had any experience with radio and with electronics. Tom replied that he knew very little about electronics, but that he had a Citizen's Band (CB) radio. He had become very unhappy with its crowded channels and tired of talking to the same people all the time. He wanted something new and exciting to do which would also be worthwhile. Louise remarked that it was obvious that he was describing ham radio, and that he would see for himself that evening.

an amateur radio station in operation

That evening, as Tom and his parents walked up to Louise's house, they were surprised and impressed by the three antennas that they could see in the yard. Tom's mother said that the yard looked like a smaller version of the local broadcasting station. One of the antennas, the one with three long metal pipes, sat up on top of a tall metal tower. Tom's father said that this antenna must be at least fifty feet high. They could also see a long thin wire running from the tower to a tree at the back of the yard. The third antenna, the one which interested them the most, was shaped like a shallow soup dish. This "dish antenna" which was larger than Tom, was at least eight feet in diameter. "Boy," Tom thought, "This one must really send out a whopper of a signal." Tom's dad said "I've read about dish antennas. They're usually used in radioastronomy to catch signals from stars. I wonder if the Grants are into UFO's?"

7

Tom, who was concentrating on the "dish," was startled by a friendly voice which said "Hello, you must be Tom." Tom looked up to see a lady whose blouse bore a bright red name tag with the words "Louise K1XXP." Tom turned to his newly met "Elmer." "Oh! Hi! Yes, Mrs. Grant, I'm Tom and these are my parents."

"Great! Nice to meet you all. Please call me Louise. Hams are very informal, Tom, and use their first names when they talk to each other. I'm so glad to see young people get their radio licenses, and I'll be very happy to help you get yours. Don't be worried about what will be strange and confusing at first. Every year, thousands of boys and girls become Novices, Technicians, Generals, Advanceds and Extras."

"What are those?" Tom's mother asked.

Louise explained that the terms Novice, Technician, General, Advanced and Extra were the names of the five basic classes of amateur radio licenses. The Novice license, which is the license class beginners usually first qualify for, allows the new operator to transmit on a rather limited number of frequencies. Novices are also limited to low power. The Technical class, although more advanced, is also limited in the radio frequencies on which they are allowed to operate. The General class license is the one which most hams hold. Although it allows hams to use a much greater range of operating frequencies and higher power, it is a step below the Advanced class. The highest and most difficult license to get is the Extra which six percent of all American amateurs, about 20,000, proudly hold. Louise added that "Even though Novices are limited in what and to whom they can talk, they have all kinds of opportunities for enjoyment as you will see."

"How difficult are the Novice tests?" Tom wanted to know. Louise explained that in order to become a Novice (which is the least difficult license to get) he would have to pass two simple tests. The first is on basic radio theory and Federal Communications Commission regulations. The second is a test of ability to send and receive Morse code at the rate of five words a minute. "Taking tests," she said, "May sound too much like school and you may begin to have second thoughts about getting involved, but these tests are so easy that very young children have passed. As a matter of fact, a four-year old recently did it. He's Neil Rapp, WB9VPG, who passed before he was five years old. Neil is a bright boy, of course, and he must have studied very hard, but he certainly showed that anyone, even a preschooler, can learn more than enough in a short time to become a licensed amateur radio operator. Charlie, my husband, and I are both Extras. You'll meet Charlie in a few minutes. Tom will be studying for his Novice test with me."

When she paused, Tom, who thought it was time to ask some more questions, asked her about all the antennas in the yard. "What do they do?" he questioned. "They certainly don't look like our TV antenna at home."

"Oh, yes, of course. TV antennas are designed for just one purpose—to receive certain radio signals. You can transmit signals with a TV antenna, but that is definitely not recommended. Our antennas are designed to work most efficiently for a few radio frequencies, both for transmitting *and* receiving. The one up on the tower is a three band beam or 'Yagi'. Yagi was the name of a Japanese scientist who first worked out the theory and design of this kind of antenna. A TV antenna, although it may not look it, is a form of 'Yagi'. Our beam is intended to receive and transmit on ten, fifteen and twenty meters, and it is mounted on a fifty foot tower.

The higher the antenna is, the better it can pick up weak signals. Since tri-banders weigh much more than TV antennas do and they have to stand up to strong winds, they are mounted on extra-strong steel or aluminum towers.''

Tom was confused. "What," he asked, "is ten, fifteen and twenty meters, and what is a beam?''

"Ten, fifteen and twenty meters are three of the radio frequencies on which General and higher class hams can operate. Meters and frequencies are not exactly the same thing, but they are closely related. You'll soon learn what they mean. Right now, I'll just say that meters refer to the distance between each radio wave sent out or received. This is called the wavelength. Frequency, on the other hand, is the number of radio waves received or sent out each second. The higher the frequency, that is, the greater the number of waves per second, the shorter the distance or wavelength between them.

"The tri-bander is called a 'beam' because it can be turned to beam or focus your radio signal in a particular direction. The principle is the same in your TV antenna if it has a rotor to turn it in any direction. When, for example, you pick up a station in England with a weak signal and you want to talk to him but your beam is focused on California, all you have to do is to turn the beam toward England. This takes only a few seconds, and you will be surprised by the way his and your signal strength increases.''

Just at that moment, the beam high above them began to turn. "Charlie is on the air right now," Louise said. "Look at the wires running from the top of the tower, one to the pole in that corner of the yard, the other to the tree in the other corner. That is also an antenna which we call an 'inverted vee'. We use it only on forty meters.''

"I thought they held the tower up," Tom confessed, a little bit abashed that he hadn't known the difference between guy wires, which help hold towers and masts in place, and a short wave antenna. "No," Louise replied, "We don't need guy wires for our tower, although free standing towers and higher towers are usually guyed. That's because we braced our tower against the side of the house. The two wires attached to the tower form a letter V turned upside down, and that's what gives this kind of antenna its name.''

Louise then turned and pointed to the long wire which ran from a tree near the house to another tree in the back. "This one," she said, "Is a dipole antenna cut to a length of 126 feet to work on a particular range of frequencies, and we use it only on 80 meters. In order for a dipole antenna to work most efficiently, it has to be just the right length. We figured out the approximate length for the frequencies we wanted to use with some simple antenna theory, and then, with some experimenting when the antenna was put up, we got just the right length. I know it all sounds terribly complicated, but it really isn't, and you'll learn all about it before you take your Novice test.''

Tom knew, of course, that he would have to take a test to become a ham, unlike CBers who don't have to take examinations in order to operate on the CB channels. He was encouraged since he remembered that one of the ARRL pamphlets which he had read had said, "Anyone with interest to become a ham can obtain a Novice license with a few weeks of study.''

"Let's go inside to the ham shack now," Louise said. "That's ham talk for operating location. With us,

it's the basement." Tom gasped in surprise when he
entered the basement to see in front of him an im-
pressive collection of electronic gear with dozens of
knobs, switches, dials and meters, some of it obviously
old while other pieces looked brand new. A large table
in one corner of the nicely-finished-off basement room
was almost completely covered with this gear, arranged
neatly on the table and on a long shelf over the table.
Tom knew that it all had to do with sending and receiving radio messages, but it seemed to be very confusing
and mysterious.

Louise saw the look of wonder and puzzlement on
Tom's face, and said in her gentlest manner, "Don't be
overwhelmed by what you see here, Tom. Remember
that we have been hams for many years, and in that
time we have built or purchased all kinds of equipment,
but we began with a few simple pieces and so will you.
That's Charlie operating right now."

Charlie, a gray-haired man, was sitting at the table
speaking into a microphone. Tom heard each word
distinctly, but nothing he heard made any sense to him.
This is what he heard: "CQ,CQ,CQ DX, this is K1XXO,
Kilowatt One, X-ray, X-ray Oscar," which was repeated
twice. Louise turned to Tom and said, "CQ is the ham's
shorthand way of inviting anyone listening to call him to
begin a QSO. QSO is an abbreviation for a two way contact. DX means foreign hams only, please, that is non-
American and non-Canadian. K1XXO is Charlie's call.
The K tells the listener that he is an American, although
W,N and A are also assigned to American hams. The 1
stands for the New England region which is where
we're located. There are ten regions in the United
States, each with its own number. California is 6, and
the southeastern states are 4. Foreign countries have
their own call letters, each assigned according to inter-

national agreement. French calls begin with F, Italian with I, Argentinian with LU and Australian with VK.''

Right after K1XXO finished his CQs, a voice with an oriental accent came into the room through the loudspeaker. Tom was thrilled to hear how clearly the voice from the loudspeaker said ''K1XXO, this is JA1VCX, Juliet, Alpha One Victor Charlie X-Ray in Tokyo.''

Tom, in a whisper, asked Louise what ''Juliet'' and ''Alpha'' meant. She replied that these words were used by hams and other radio operators to emphasize their call letters and names. ''Many foreign hams,'' she said, ''speak little English, and atmospheric conditions may make it difficult to understand what they are saying. For these reasons, hams use the system of tying an internationally-agreed-on word to each letter of the alphabet. For example, it is often hard to know whether a ham is saying 'B' or 'V,' but these letters are easily recognized as 'Bravo' and 'Victor'.'' Louise stressed the importance of clear, deliberate speech, particularly when talking to DX stations.

As Tom turned back to the QSO in progress, he suddenly realized that Charlie was actually talking to a ham in Tokyo, many thousands of miles away. Tokyo, just like that! Great! JA1VCX was just saying to Charlie in a slow, precise way, ''You have a fine signal here in Tokyo, the capital city of Japan. My name is Toshi, I spell, Tango, Oscar, Sierra, Hotel, India, Toshi. Your signal report is a 5 by 6, 5 by 6, very little QRM, but some QRN. My rig is a Yaesu FT-901DM, 180 watts input, and the antenna is a three element Yagi. I'll say 73s to you now, my friend Charlie, because many others are calling me. Good luck and best wishes to you and your family. K1XXO, this is JA1VCX. Over.''

---

[1]See ''The Meaning of Call Letters'' and ''Districts and Representative Calls in the United States,'' Appendix, p. 73 and 74.

"Roger, Toshi. JA1CVX from K1XXO. Fine business and thank you very much for this fine QSO. I will send you a QSL card and would very much appreciate receiving one from you. 73. This is K1XXO. Clear."

"73, Charlie. This is JA1CVX clear, and QRZ stateside?"

"Hello" Charlie said as he turned around to meet Tom and his parents. "That was a phone, SSB or single-side band, transmission. To talk with a microphone the way I just did, you have to hold a General or higher class license."

"Charlie, what did you and Toshi mean by 'clear', and what was QRZ and QRM and 5 by 6 and," the words came tumbling out in Tom's eagerness, "where can I operate and to whom can I talk when I'm a Novice?"

"One thing at a time, Tom. Clear means that the operator has finished his or her end of the QSO. QRZ is an abbreviation for "Who is calling me?" QRM and QRN, which Toshi used, are abbreviations for interference and noise. QRM is caused by hams and nearby frequencies. QRN is a natural interference from static and other atmospheric noises."

"As a Novice, Tom, you can operate on certain parts of the 80, 40, 15 and 10 meter bands. I'm sure that you're disappointed by not being able to go on phone until you have your General ticket, but code operation is a lot of fun, and many hams prefer it by far to phone. Louise and I divide our time up equally with these two transmission modes. Right now, I'll—Oh, yes, you also asked about the meaning of 5 by 6. Most ham receivers have a signal strength meter which we read to give us the signal strength of the signal we're listening to. The numbers used range from a 1 which means faint, barely heard signals to a 9 which is a very strong signal. Toshi said my signal strength was a 6 which is a good report.

The other number, the 5, refers to the quality and audibility of the signal. The 5 Toshi gave me meant that my transmissions were perfectly understandable and of excellent quality. A 1, on the other hand, means that even though the signal may be loud, the quality is so bad that it cannot be understood.''

"I think that you have probably had enough of these terms, Tom, so I'll go back on the air for a CW QSO since this will be how you will operate for some time.'' As Charlie turned the transceiver tuning dial, Tom heard the strangest variety of sounds coming out of the speaker—high pitched dots and dashes, static, weak ''rushing'' noises, and voices speaking, more or less clearly, in languages that Tom could not understand.

Charlie explained that amateur transmitters were very different from CB sets, a fact that Tom already knew. "Hams," Charlie said, "are not restricted to 40 crowded frequencies, but can operate on the entire frequency ranges assigned to them. For example, the 20 meter band which is the one I'm on now, and is the best all around DX band, has a frequency range of 14.000 to 14.350 megahertz, or 14,000,000 to 14,350,000 radio waves each second. Compare these frequencies with the FM frequencies which run from 88 megahertz to 108 megahertz. You know these FM numbers because you see them on your FM dial. Our local FM station is on the 103.5 megahertz frequency which is a much higher frequency than the 14 megahertz I'm on now."

Charlie added that on the VHF or very high frequencies, 144 megahertz and up, on which hams can operate, "channelized" transmitters and receivers are often used, but channels are very restrictive. With the rapid advances in electronic engineering, "synthesized" transceivers which cover an entire VHF band are now on the market. As a result, hams who have purchased one of these new "rigs" are able to work on an almost unlimited number of frequencies on 144 megahertz. "Now," he said, "I'll go on code so that you will have some idea of what it's about even though you won't know what is being said. I'll call CQ now."

Tom had heard the rhythmic sound of Morse code dots and dashes before. War movies almost always had a scene in which a radio operator was seen and heard sending and receiving code messages, but he had never before thought about the possibility of learning to use the code himself. The dots and dashes he now heard (the sound was more like dits and dahs than dots and dashes) sounded much like those he had listened to before—fast beeps that he didn't understand. As he stood watching Charlie with some awe, he had no idea that in a few months he too would be able to copy and understand those strange sounds with some ease.

Louise, however, knew what was to come as long as Tom was reasonably diligent in practicing sending and receiving code. She commented that "It won't be long, Tom, before you'll copy all of that without missing a word. Code becomes a language you will use almost as well as you use English now. Hams usually include the International Morse Code as one of their languages. Of course, its structure, tenses and grammar are always in the language of the ham sending it. As you go along, you will quickly pick up the many convenient abbreviations which are internationally used."[2]

Charlie, who had just finished his CW QSO broke in. "The importance of code can't be overemphasized. You have to know the code even if you intend to operate exclusively on phone. Years ago, in the '20's

---

[2] See "Common CW Abbreviations" and "Q Signals", Appendix, p. 77-79.

and '30's, hams generally operated CW only. Even today, many hams prefer cw operating. Whenever there is a lot of QRM or QRN, it is much easier to hear and copy cw signals than phone signals. Let's talk about a possible trouble situation in which a ham is on a small boat in a storm. He's losing electrical power, and his signal is so weak that you can hardly hear his voice. If he can switch to CW, his signals will be sharper and have a penetrating pitch which SSB signals lack, and listeners can catch his distress calls much more easily. This is important in emergencies, and since hams are public-spirited and give their services freely in emergencies, it's obvious that they should be expert in code.''

Louise pointed to the top of the table at which Charlie was sitting. ''See those pieces of equipment, Tom? They're called 'keys'. They don't resemble each other very much, but they are used to send code. This one is a straight key. That's the one Charlie just used and it's the one everyone recognizes. It's also the kind that you will learn on. The one next to it is an 'automatic' keyer which we use for very fast sending. The third one is a semi-automatic 'bug' which was very popular years ago, and the fourth is a keyboard sender which looks like a typewriter. As I said, you'll begin with a straight key—the others are designed for experienced amateurs.''

Charlie shut off the rig, and as he gave Tom one of his QSL cards, he shook Tom's hand and said ''Welcome to the fellowship of hams, Tom. Louise will tell you what to do now to get ready for the Novice license. I'll be happy to help at any time, but it's Louise who is your ''Elmer'' and she will give you all the help you need to become a Novice now and a General later. You'll have to do some studying, of course. After all, you will have to take the license test yourself, and then be on your own as an operating ham. Louise will be available, however, to smooth out some of the rough spots."

Tom thanked Louise and Charlie, and after arranging a time for his first tutoring session, he and his parents started out for home. Tom's mind was whirling with all that he had seen and heard. He knew now that he wanted to become a ham more than he wanted anything else in his life, and he was determined that it wouldn't take him very long to join the fellowship to which he had been invited by Charlie.

As we leave Tom now with his thoughts about his newly-discovered hobby, we will turn to the many fascinating aspects of amateur radio about which he will learn—the organization of the amateur radio field, the nature of the tests which must be taken, the kinds of equipment suitable for Novices, the details of setting up a ham station, and the kinds of activities in which hams participate and the resources available to them.

3 getting your license

THE FEDERAL COMMUNICATION COMMISSION

Everyone has heard the old saying that "The air is free." Air to breathe is free, but is is *not* free for transmitting radio waves. By international agreement, radio stations and radio operators must be licensed by their governments. The need for licensing became evident soon after radio or as it was then known, "wireless telegraphy," become popular. The air waves became so overcrowded with transmission of all kinds—commercial, military and amateur—that governments decided that the "air" was their national property to be used only with governmental permission. The operation of radio transmitters was restricted to people who passed licensing tests and could prove that they had a good reason for sending wireless messages.

19

Since radio waves pass easily and quickly over international boundaries, concerned nations formed the International Telecommunications Union, whose present membership now numbers more than 150 countries. Regulations approved by the International Telecommunications Union form the basis for international control of all radio frequencies. Member nations accept the decisions of the ITU as to the frequencies each uses and the purpose for which they are used, so that radio transmitters in one country will not seriously interfere with radio reception in another country, or even in the same country. You have often heard radio stations interfering with each other, and have seen results when a television station in Los Angeles interferes with another station in San Francisco, or a Boston station "wipes out" a New York station when both are operating on the same frequency.

The United States Congress created a regulatory agency, the Federal Communications Commission (FCC) which, operating under the International Telecommunications Union rules and authorizing legislation by Congress, is responsible for all radio transmission, commercial, amateur, military, citizen's band, and public service. The FCC, sometimes called the "Friendly Candy Company" by hams, assigns specific radio and television frequencies to licensed users. Individuals who operate radio and television stations, with some exceptions such as Citizen's Band and certain public services, must pass licensing examinations. Transmitting stations must also be licensed.

The competition for transmitting frequencies is intense since available freqencies are limited, and commercial and military applications are increasing. In this competition, radio amateurs would seem to be at a great disadvantage, but because they have proved their value to the nation so often and also because they were using the air waves long before the FCC was established, they have been assigned to a number of frequencies of their own. This assignment has just been reconfirmed by the latest World Administrative Conference of the ITU held in 1979.[1]

The FCC has recognized the importance of amateur radio in these words:

The rules and regulations in this part [of the FCC U.S. Amateur Regulations] are designed to provide an amateur radio service having a fundamental purpose as expressed in the following principles:

a). Recognition and enhancement of the value of the amateur service to the public as a voluntary non-commercial communication service, particularly with respect to providing emergency communications.

b). Continuation and extension of the amateur's proven service through rules which provide for advancing skills in both communication and technical phases of the art.

c). Encouragement and improvement of the amateur radio service through rules which provide for advancing skills in both communication and technical phases of the art.

d). Continuation and extension of the amateur's unique ability to enhance international good will.

You are already aware of the assistance radio operators give in emergencies and of the "enhancement of good will" through DX contacts, but part b) above is just as important. Many of the advances in radio which have become part of the electronics industry were first made by hams who were primarily interested in improv-

---

[1]See "The Story of Call Signs," Appendix, p. 73.

ing their own equipment. Radio amateurs, for example, first demonstrated that reliable radio communication was practical with low power on short wave frequencies, and that the antennas and radio circuits which they designed for this purpose were more effective than expensive, commercially-designed sets. Many radio operators have become professional radio engineers and radio officers because of the skills they developed in their hobby. Today, as in the past, many amateurs work in the electronics industry, combining, as it were, both business and pleasure.

FCC LICENSE TESTS FOR AMATEURS

Now, how can *you* become a radio amateur? How can you get started in this fascinating hobby? As you already know, you must pass a special licensing examination which tests your grasp of FCC rules and radio theory. In addition, you must show that you can send and receive the International Morse Code at a rate of five words per minute. The written Novice examination is designed to find out if the license applicant knows the correct principles and practices of operating an amateur station in accordance with the conditions that apply to that license class. As soon as the applicant is informed that he or she has passed the examination, the new Novice is legally authorized to talk to hams all over the world with the International Morse Code with a power of up to 250 watts, on the frequencies specifically set aside for Novice operation.

Passing examinations may sound like a difficult task, but thousands of men and women, boys and girls, from five to eighty-five years of age, qualify every year.

Novices and individuals without licenses who already know radio theory and application on a more advanced level and are able to send and receive code at the rate of 13 words per minute are encouraged to take the examination for the popular General class license. You don't have to be a licensed ham in order to take the General class tests, and many hams have started as Generals. Indeed, there are cases of well-qualified people who have taken and passed the General, Advanced and Extra class tests in a single day.

General class privileges are better than Novice class privileges since more frequencies are open to Generals who may also operate radio-telephony (phone) in addition to CW. The Technician class is limited to the very high frequencies (VHF), above 50.0 MHz. The Advanced class has still more operating frequencies, while the Extra, a ticket held only by six percent of the 300,000 licensed American hams, confers the greatest number of operating privileges. Because it requires the most proficiency in code, radio theory and radio operation, the Extra class license is the highest and most prestigious of all.

Like Tom Sachs and most beginners in amateur radio, you will probably begin as a Novice. Novice tests are the most convenient to take because they are ordinarily given by a volunteer examiner who must be General Class or higher. Most hams, like Louise who was Tom Sachs' "Elmer," are eager to help beginners get ready for the tests. As soon as your "Elmer" or class instructor thinks you are ready, he or she will give you the code test of twenty-five five letter groups transmitted at the rate of five words per minute. To pass, you must copy at least 25 consecutive letters correctly. That is, you must copy one full minute of the code message without error. You will also be tested on how well you can send code at the rate of five words per minute without serious error.[1]

Children and teenagers quickly learn to send and receive code, and it rarely takes long for them to be ready for the code examination. Then, as soon as you and your "Elmer" or class instructor think you are ready for the written examination, he or she will fill out an FCC application form, FCC form 610, which certifies that the examiner is eligible to give the written theory and application test, and that you have passed the code test. In a few weeks, your examiner will receive the Novice examination from the FCC. This is a 20 question multiple-choice test which you take in the examiner's presence. Since the answer sheet must be returned for correcting to the FCC, you will have to wait a few weeks before you learn how well you did. Fifteen out of the twenty questions must be correctly answered in order to pass. If you pass, and most Novice applicants *do* pass, you will know because one glorious day you will find in the mail an envelope from the FCC which contains your new Novice license with your own call letters.

Page 87-89 in the appendix gives ten sample questions like those on the Novice test. Several can be answered correctly just from what you learn in this book. The topics on which the Novice test is based are listed in the Appendix, page 83-89.

WA1UAW, the junior author of this book, received his Novice license on his 13th birthday, which made it a doubly exciting and pleasurable day. You will be the only person in the world who holds your particular call. The license, which the FCC requires that you sign and

---

[1]"The Ham Radio Morse Code" see Appendix, page 73.

post prominently in your "shack" when you first go on the air, serves as both a station and operator's license.

Should you fail the written examination, you must wait thirty days before applying to take it again. But, as we have already said, few people fail the Novice tests. Although most Novices begin to prepare for the General class license almost as soon as they have passed their Novice test, there is really no need to rush since the Novice license is valid for five years and may be renewed without examination for additional five-year terms. However, few Novices remain for very long as Novices since their operating privileges are so limited.

Although "Elmers" and special courses are available in many towns and cities to help Novices study for the next test, many amateurs have discovered they are fully capable of learning enough by themselves. When you think you are ready for the General tests, that is, when you are confident that you can send and receive 13 words per minute in code without difficulty (you should be able to copy and send 15 words per minute so as to be extra sure), and when you have mastered the somewhat more advanced sections of rules, electronic theory and practice on which you will be examined, you should apply for the General class test.

Incidentally, many Novices discover that while it is rather easy to increase their code speed to about 10 words per minute, they get stuck at this speed and can't raise it. This learning "plateau" is a temporary block and will be surmounted before long. Some unfortunate hams, however, remain on that plateau for weeks or even months, but this frustration is uncommon, and young boys and girls usually move ahead very quickly.

Many learning aids for increasing code speed are available. One of the best is to listen to W1AW, the ARRL station in Newington, Connecticut which operates on many frequencies and times during the day and night sending perfect code at speeds from 3½, 5, 7½, 10, 13, 15, 20, 25 and even higher speeds per minute. In addition, the ARRL, *73* Magazine, and a number of commercial suppliers have produced tape code cassettes and records which have helped thousands of hams improve their code speed.

The ARRL will, on request, send a schedule of its code transmissions on receipt of a stamped self-addressed envelope.

Since boys and girls learn code quickly, this part of the General class hurdle will soon be overcome. The more difficult task will probably be the more advanced electronic theory and its applications to amateur radio. Since the Novice test is the only one which can be given at home by a volunteer examiner, you will have to make an appointment at a conveniently-located FCC testing point for the General class examination. In many of the twenty-nine large cities where FCC Field Offices are maintained, appointments are not usually necessary, but you will need to know the day and time on which to appear. In Los Angeles, examinations for General class licenses are regularly scheduled at 8:30 A.M. and 1:00 P.M. daily. In Chicago, they are given at 8:45 A.M. every Friday; in Boston, at 9:00 A.M. on Wednesday. Many hams live too far away from the Field Offices and as a convenience to them, the FCC schedules examination days two to four times a year at some seventy other cities around the country. The very large state of Texas has established such testing sites at Austin, Corpus Christi, El Paso, Lubbock and San Antonio in addition to its official Field Offices in Beaumont, Dallas and Houston.

Schedules and addresses of FCC Field Offices are listed in the ARRL publication, *The Radio Amateur's*

License Manual, which is revised every year to keep up to date. This and other ARRL publications are available by mail order from ARRL headquarters and in many bookstores and libraries.

Appointments must be made well in advance with the FCC in order to be approved to take your test at one of these additional test centers. All you have to do is to fill out FCC form 610 which is available free of charge from the nearest FCC Field Office, or from ARRL headquarters if you send them a stamped self-addressed envelope. Your local ham club and your "Elmer" often have a supply of these forms on hand. Send the completed application to the FCC Field Engineer at a conveniently-located Field Office. Shortly before the scheduled day, you will receive a permission notice from the FCC, giving the time and location to which to report.

Don't be surprised when you find a large crowd of hams waiting on the day that you report. Ham radio is very popular and many hams strive to move up to the higher licenses. You may be interested in the fact that there are more than 47,000 hams in California, more than 24,000 in New York State and more than 19,500 in Texas, and many of them are ready to upgrade. We have taken our tests with as many as forty people crowded into one room. Once the FCC examiner has checked everyone's permission slips, and has determined which tests they are to take, the examinations begin. Those hams who are scheduled for the General class test will be seated together for the 13-word per-minute code test which they must pass first. As soon as everyone is ready, the Examiner will play a special code cassette for the waiting group. You will probably not be taking the once-mandatory five-minute code message of which you had to copy one full minute of text without error.

Instead, you will only need to answer eight or more questions correctly on the ten-question multiple-choice test which is designed to show how well you understand the five-minute message.

The Examiner will score the answer sheets quickly and tell all applicants whether or not they have passed. Those who pass (and, unfortunately some do fail because of nervousness or simply because they were not ready) will soon be seated for the theory and applicatons test which consists of fifty multiple-choice questions. The lowest passing mark on this test is 37 correct answers or 74%. About two-thirds of the General Class questions are on radio theory and application. The remainder are on general operating procedure and FCC rules.

You may think that all of this sounds like a real ordeal just to become a General class amateur, and you may be wondering why you should get involved with what may seem to be a great diversion of time and a lot of hard work when you may not even pass the examination. Many thousands of boys and girls have asked this question. It is obvious that most have answered it positively—after all, the number of young people in amateur radio has grown enormously in recent years. There are many good reasons for making the effort. These new Generals, like you, were eager to communicate with other young men and women around the world. They, like you, could have exercised their option—to stay with the Novice ticket with its real limitations, or even give it all up and return to Citizen's Band radio where there are no examinations and no radio theory to learn. But, there is very little real communication in CB, and what there is is very limited. Particularly in heavily populated areas, CB is a jungle of competing voices, voices fighting vainly to be heard. The legal power limit of five watts input, often disregarded by CB "outlaws," keeps the distance over which one may communicate to a minimum.

Compare this with the advantages of radio amateur communication which, as a Novice, you will already know. Amateurs may use an almost infinitely greater number of radio frequencies, and since there are many fewer amateurs competing for clear frequencies, your chances of making many good contacts are almost always very good. To be fair, there are times, in the evening, on weekends and during DX contests when every possible frequency seems to be in use and you may have to use an "electronic shoe horn" to make your contacts.

Novices may use up to 250 watts of input power, *fifty* times more than the legal CB limit; General and higher class hams may run as much as 1000 watts input. In short, as a General class ham, you will have many more opportunities for communicating than you do as a Novice; a few miles on the very high frequencies of 144-148 MHz (2 meters); hundreds of miles or more on 3.65 (80 meters) and 7.15 (40 meters) MHZ, and around the world on 14.050 (20 meters) and 21.150 (15 meters) MHz.

If, like so many boys and girls, you are especially interested in testing electrical circuits and in electronic experimentation, you will have already learned that opportunities for experimentation in ham radio are limitless. Hams are engaged in an enormously varied range of experimental activities from building simple receivers and transmitters to sponsoring two earth-circling satellites designed for new modes of communication. These satellites are named OSCAR, which is an acronym, a name formed from the first letters of the words in their descriptive title. This title is Orbiting

Satellite Carrying Amateur Radio. The OSCAR's are intended to rebroadcast signals from amateurs over a much greater area than is regularly possible by standard transmission. Special kinds of antennas, some like the "dish" antenna which Tom Sachs first saw in Louise's yard, are used since satellites move with great speed, and OSCAR is in range at any one location for fifteen minutes or less. The "dish" antenna is focused on the region of the sky through which the satellite will pass, and excellent results have been obtained by thousands of hams in the few years in which the OSCAR's have circled the earth.

Other kinds of antennas may also be tested, and nearly every issue of the ham magazines will describe some new design. Not every amateur finds this kind of experimentation to be his or her special interest, but that is one of the joys of the hobby—you can pick and choose from many absorbing activities. For example, some hams have gotten into "moonbounce" communication. In "moonbounce," you aim a specially designed antenna at the moon. Your signal is reflected from the moon's surface back to earth, to be picked up and answered by hams far away from you. Many contacts are regularly made via "moonbounce." "Moonbounce," however, is not an easy mode of communication because it calls for high power, sensitive receivers, well-constructed antennas and accurate aim.

One of the most popular ham activities is public service. There are countless opportunities in amateur radio for public service. Hams have always been on hand during emergencies in which they provide essential communication links for police, Red Cross, and Civil Defense by transmitting vital information during floods, storms, electrical power disruptions and fires.

Hams also participate by the thousands in the many networks (nets) which pass messages within and between states. They provide a very important service which is, unfortunately, not very well known to the general public. Suppose that a friend wishes to send a message to someone living thousands of miles away. If you are a member of a local net, you can transmit that message during the regularly-scheduled net period on an agreed upon frequency. A designated member of the net will relay it to an interstate net, and, soon after, a ham in the distant town will read the message over the telephone to the addressee. If the message cannot be telephoned, the receiving ham will deliver it to the local address, usually typed on a special form. This is a free service since amateurs are not permitted to receive pay for these services. Most nets operate on frequencies which are not open to Novices, but as soon as Novices upgrade to a higher license class, they will be welcome to participate. It may be of interest to note that the Amateur Radio Relay League took its name from these message relays.

"Phone patching" is another of the fascinating aspects of the wonderful world of amateur radio. In "phone patching," a simple kind of electronic coupler is connected to the telephone and persons calling via ham radio from outside the country can be connected through your receiver and telephone to a friend or relative living near you. Once you have heard a call for a "phone patch" to your area, and have established voice contact with the transmitting station, you dial the telephone number given by the calling party (reversing the charge if it is a long distance call). When the receiving party is on the telephone, you switch the foreign caller's voice into the phone line, and the radio-telephone contact between the distant caller and the receiving party can go ahead. "Phone patching" is a routine operation for many hams. Passengers or crew members sailing on ships on which there happens to be an amateur operator (many radio operators on shipboard are hams) often take advantage of this free service. The most spectacular "phone patch" and the one which has given your authors the greatest pleasure is "phone patching" calls from the American Antarctic team near the South Pole, some 10,000 miles away, with their families in the States.

Still other kinds of experimental communication which interest hams are television (SSTV or Slow Scan Television) by which hams see as well as talk to each other, and RTTY (Radio-Teletype). One of the intriguing developments in RTTY is the RTTY receiver-printer which automatically turns itself on when a message on the proper frequency is received. The RTTY printer then prints the message on a sheet of paper. Although commercially manufactured SSTV and RTTY equipment especially designed for amateur use is on the market, most hams who experiment with these two modes of communication build much of their gear, adapting commercial equipment as necessary, and constructing whatever else is needed.

Amateurs have a lot of fun participating in the activities described above, but they probably look forward most of all to the annual "Field Day" weekend late in June sponsored by the ARRL. Thousands of hams all over the world plan eagerly for "Field Day," laying in ample supplies of food and drink, electronic gear, tents and the other necessary supplies for the hectic weekend to come.

The purpose of "Field Day" is to encourage hams to build and use equipment which does not depend on regular electric power. "Field Day" serves as a valuable preparation for those emergency situations during which commercial electric power is unavailable. The hundreds of radio clubs which participate usually depend on portable electrical generators and batteries, although bicycle power is occasionally found, and solar-powered sources are becoming more popular.

As a rule, clubs try to locate a suitable high point for "Field Day," although they will set up wherever they can find suitable space if they have to. They erect their antennas and arrange their transmitters and receivers before the starting time so that precious time will be saved for the race to make contacts. The hams work in shifts around the clock to make as many CW and phone contacts as possible during the weekend on as many bands as feasible. They keep detailed logs of all contacts and wait with keen anticipation for the results which will be announced by the ARRL a few months later after the ARRL staff has had a chance to check the hundreds of logs sent in by the clubs. Points are awarded for each contact, the number of points depending on the country or state worked, the power used, the number of bands, as well as a number of other factors.

At the end of the "Field Day," the weary but happy hams dismantle their equipment and return to their homes to begin planning for the next "Field Day" weekend.

The challenge of amateur radio and the opportunities for enjoyment and self-improvement through the amateur radio are virtually endless. *That* is why so many young people have worked to pass the various license examinations. They are eager and happy to get involved. No matter what their or your interest is—meeting other hams on phone or CW, experimenting with circuits and equipment, handling messages as net members, or serving their communities in emergencies, amateur radio has something to offer everyone.

Taking tests and putting together an amateur radio station is obviously not play. Determined effort and study *are* required, but, as you know, anything *worth* doing requires effort and study, and there are many "Elmers" and all kinds of helpful materials to make the task less difficult. The personal reward, as hundreds of thousands of hams have discovered for themselves during the seventy or more years of amateur radio's existence, *is* well worth the effort.

4
getting
on the air

WHERE TO PUT
YOUR HAM SHACK

Once your Novice license arrives, you'll want to get on the air as soon as possible. Fortunately, all it takes is a few pieces of equipment which can be set up almost anywhere—an apartment, for example, although apartments often limit or even forbid outside antennas, in a one or two family house, in a trailer—indeed, in just about any habitable area with electric power. Even if the little space needed for a station is not available, or if money to purchase equipment is short, you may be able to use your local club station. Since some clubs do not have their own stations, you may still be able to arrange for some operating sessions at your "Elmer's" shack or with another local ham.

35

If you can operate at home, the station will usually materialize in the attic or the basement. Attics are usually too hot in summer and too cold in winter, and electric power for your rig may not be available unless a new electric line is run into the attic. This is often a reasonably inexpensive job. Temperatures in basements, on the other hand, tend to stay more even, and basements generally have better access. More important, however, good electrical grounds such as copper or iron water pipes which are necessary for proper operation of electrical equipment and personal safety, are more likely to be available. Basements often suffer from high summer humidity, a condition which can be quickly eliminated with an inexpensive dehumidifier, and from the need to run an antenna connection all the way down to the basement. If the basement is unfinished, it may be dark and dusty, but these drawbacks have not stopped most amateurs in the past. It is particularly important to locate your shack near the best ground connections, and as near as possible to the place where the lead-in cable from your antenna (or, as you will soon discover, antennas) will enter the room. Of course, you will need a table or desk like the one Louise and Charlie used, the larger the better, on which to set your receiver and transmitter and other gear. Nearby, there should be a workplace for tools and storage and for the many radio parts and pieces of equipment that seem to multiply as time passes.

SELECTING YOUR EQUIPMENT

Even before you decide on where to locate the station, you will be thinking and dreaming about your equipment. The capability and quality of this equipment will naturally depend on how much you can spend. Since boys and girls usually have little money for equipment, your best buy may well be used equipment. Although prices may vary from dealer to dealer, a used transceiver will usually sell for $200 to $300 dollars less than a new transceiver. For example, if the new Drake TR-4C transceiver sells for $700, it will be about $450 used. Earlier models such as the TR-4B and TR-4 will perhaps be $50 to $150 less. The Kenwood TS-520SE, at about $650 new will, in its earlier models, be $150 to $200 less. Prices may vary widely, however, depending on popularity of the model, production cost increases, condition, and even, with imported equipment, the exchange rate of the Yen and the dollar.

Since Novices may not transmit with more than 250 watts of input power, don't buy a higher-powered transmitter unless you expect to move up to the General class in the near future and will want higher power. Many hams are completely satisfied with power levels of about 200 watts input which is the power input capability of most new transmitters. Ham radio stores usually sell used equipment which has been traded in by hams for new equipment. The dealer services and warrantees these transmitters and receivers for a limited period, usually 30 days. This equipment is generally in good-to-better "used" condition and will work well. Your "Elmer" may even know of a local ham who wishes to sell some of his or her equipment. This can be a very good buy if the equipment appears to have been given reasonable care. One good thing about buying equipment from a local ham is that the seller knows its problems, and can instruct the beginner in its operation. Don't buy equipment from private sellers unless you have a chance to see it in operation and to run it your-self first.

Many hams begin with used equipment and then "trade up" as they become more expert and need better equipment. The advertisements for new and used equipment in the ham radio magazines, *QST, CQ, Ham Radio Horizons, 73 Magazine,* and *Ham Radio,* are eagerly scanned by hams in the market for new or better rigs. However, one must be cautious in buying used equipment by mail order, unless it is new and war-ranteed. Many hams, however, do buy from ads, and are usually happy with their purchases.

Ham Radio Horizons which is the only ham maga-zine written specifically for the ham radio newcomer often runs articles on buying used and new equipment. Most of the magazines regularly test new equipment and report their results for all to read.[3] These reviews can be very helpful in making a decision about what to buy.

New factory or store-warranteed gear is more likely to be trouble-free, although new equipment, es-pecially if it is one of the first models coming off the production line, can have problems. Modern radio equipment is more and more likely to be entirely solid state, that is, all vacuum tubes have been eliminated. These sets, although a miracle of small size and ease of operation, are too difficult for most home repairs. When there is trouble, the set must be returned to the store or to the manufacturer. Usually, however, the rig turns out to be relatively trouble-free and will work for years without difficulty.

Purchasing a transmitter is complicated by the fact that you will have to decide on either a transceiver which is a combined *trans*mitter-re*ceiver* on one chassis, or a separate receiver and transmitter. The

---

[3] "*Ham Radio Horizons* announced in October, 1980 that it will now be written for general and advanced class hams as well as for novices."

transceiver is smaller and is usually costs less than the individual units cost. This is because both the transmitter and transceiver sections of the transceiver use many common circuit connections and parts. Transceivers can go on the air very quickly. All you need to do is to connect the transceiver (once it is unpacked, that is) to a proper antenna, a good ground and a CW key. One dial of the transceiver controls both receiving and transmitting frequencies. Let's say that you decide to send on 3.745MHz (Novices operate on the frequencies between 3.700 and 3.750MHz on the 80 meter band). Tuning the transceiver to 3.745MHz sets the receiving *and* transmitting frequencies at the same time.

If you choose to go the route of the separate receiver-transmitter, the two pieces of equipment must be connected, and antenna and ground connections made as with a transceiver. Then, when on the air, the operator must carefully match the receiver frequency with the transmitter frequency. Although this is more inconvenient than transceiver operation, the individual units are more flexible since you can listen on one frequency and send on another. This is called "split-frequency" operation, and is very useful in chasing DX when foreign stations are on frequencies not open to American hams.

If you decide to buy the separate units, you will then have to choose between a "general coverage" receiver which covers all the radio frequencies between 1.8MHz and 30MHz, and a "ham-band" only receiver which, as the name says, covers only the regular ham bands. The latter is much easier to tune since the divisions on the dial are larger and more easily read. It is also more efficient electronically because the many electrical circuits are designed to work on only a few frequencies. The wider coverage of the "general coverage'' receiver is an asset in the ham shack because you will be able to tune in foreign broadcasters, aircraft, ships and other transmissions on non-ham frequencies.

Many hams own both kinds of receivers, one for ham business, the other for broader coverage and as a spare in case of trouble with their primary receiver.

Much has been written about the merits of the different kinds of tuning systems, and hams will argue about the most efficient tuning system. Several are in use. All work well, and, depending on price, there may be little to choose between them, providing that the tuning mechanism is undamaged, and that it turns freely without binding or sticking. The circular dial tuner may take a little more time to master than the sliderule type, but the difference is trivial. Nearly all of the new receivers and transceivers use circular dials or, as an available option, offer instant automatic digital frequency readout for a hundred dollars, more or less. This means that as your receiver or transceiver is tuned, the frequency is clearly displayed in numbers, usually to an accuracy of four or more decimal places, i.e., 14.3279 MHz or 3.5091MHz. Within a few years, all ham band transceivers, receivers and transmitters will come equipped from the factory with digital readout excepting perhaps for a few economy models, and even these lower-priced models will have digital readout options.

As a rule, the more the receiver costs, the better its quality and the higher its selectivity and sensitivity. Receiver selectivity and sensitivity are extremely important for good reception. Lower-priced receivers are usually forced to skimp on the circuits and components which give high selectivity and sensitivity. Sensitivity is defined as the ease with which weak signals can be picked up and made intelligible. Sensitive receivers catch and amplify weak signals without the excessive noise and distortion of less sensitive receivers which leave weak signals "in the mud"; that is, the signals are masked by atmospheric noise and noise produced inside the receiver itself.

Selectivity, on the other hand, is the ease with which a signal on a certain frequency is clearly and sharply separated from another signal which is very close in frequency. Selectivity is probably the more important characteristic for the Novice because Novice bands tend to be crowded. It is not weak signals which are the concern of the Novice operator, but rather the fact that loud signals may be so close to each other that they are difficult to separate. That is why good receiver selectivity is so important. Unfortunately, it is not easy to decide how selective and sensitive receivers are from their advertising literature. Hams in the market for a used or new receiver try to find other hams who know the models under consideration; they read the critical product reports in the ham magazines; they talk to dealers. In short, they investigate thoroughly before buying. Although price alone does not necessarily determine quality, it *is* a good indicator. However, as a Novice or even higher class ham, you may never use many of the features of a high-priced set, and you may not wish to pay a premium price for them.

Although there is little you can do to improve the sensitivity of a receiver, it is possible to add a purchased or "home-brewed" device called a "pre-amplifier" which will increase the strength of the signal before it feeds into the receiver. Many hams have improved the capability of their receivers with pre-amplifiers at a relatively low cost.

Selectivity can be improved remarkably with a special filter. For CW operation, the elimination of signals more than 200 Hertz above or below your operating frequency is very helpful in reducing interference. CW signals are usually quite sharp, and since they take up so little space on the dial, it is important to focus in sharply on them. Receivers designed primarily for cw have built-in narrow pass band filters. That is, they filter out the competing signals and permit only the signal which is right on your listening frequency to "pass." If, however, you intend to spend a lot of time on phone operation, that is, when you become a General, you will need a receiver with a much broader filter since speech requires broad frequencies to be intelligible. Fortunately, even though the human voice ranges from a few hundred Hertz to 15,000 Hertz in frequency, from the bass to the high soprano, speech which is limited to 200 to 3000 Hertz is intelligible. Even this restricted voice range takes up more than 6 times the CW band width.

The best receivers build in a varity of filters which, at the flip of a switch, may either be used for CW or phone. Low priced receivers, on the other hand, usually offer only one filter which is most likely to be best for phone. However, inexpensive cw filters are readily available from several manufacturers. These filters are quickly connected to any receiver and noticeably improve selectivity.

TRANSMITTERS

Years ago, Novices were severely limited by the FCC to a small number of operating frequencies. For example, their transmitters had to be crystal-controlled which meant that Novices could operate only on the frequencies for which they had crystals. If the Novice could afford 6 crystals, he or she could operate on only six frequencies instead of all frequencies in the Novice bands.

   Scientists discovered many years ago that specially cut quartz crystals are resonant at certain frequencies, and vibrate at those frequencies. These frequencies depend on the thickness, length and the way in which the crystal is sliced, and they can be used in the transmitter to control the frequency of the radio waves generated. Radio crystals are usually sealed in metal containers which may be quickly plugged into or removed from the circuit in order to change the operating frequency. The advantage of crystal control is that transmitters can be held to a predetermined frequency much more easily than with other means of control. The greatest disadvantage, particularly from the point of view of the ham, is that every time he or she wants to move up or down the band, the crystal must be changed. A Novice whose only crystal is cut for 7.125MHz would call CQ on that frequency, and then hurriedly tune the receiver through the Novice portion of the band searching for another Novice who may have heard the 7.125MHz transmission, but can only answer on, let us say, 7.139MHz.

   Crystal-controlled-transmitters are still available at low prices, and may be rather good buys because, unlike the situation in the past, Novices who hear your signal on 7.125MHz or whatever crystal frequencies you may have, will probably not be crystal-controlled and can quickly come back to you right on 7.125MHz. You can't move from the location, but the other ham can. If you are unfortunate enough to be swallowed up by QRM, there is nothing you can do about it. You are stuck on that frequency unless you have another crystal. The best buy for the new Novice will probably *not* be a crystal-controlled set, but rather a newer (and more expensive) transmitter with a built in VFO, variable frequency oscillator, which is what enables non-crystal-controlled transmitters to change frequency with a turn of the dial.

Crystals are nearly obsolete in Novice transmitters, but they have many uses in modern radio work. They are in everyday use in very high frequency radio, VHF, such as the two meter band where the very popular hand-held "walkie-talkie" transceiver has five to six frequencies, each controlled by crystals. The latest two meter rigs have done away with crystals, although at a higher cost, and with their advanced electronics, are now fully "synthesized," which means that they can receive and transmit on hundreds of frequencies without crystals.

Depending on finances, then, you can start with a good used transceiver for cw and phone operation at a price hundreds of dollars below that of a new transceiver, or you can buy a new economy rig, lacking many of the special features of the better sets, at a cost comparable to that of used equipment. If you know how to solder and are familiar with practical electronics, you may even build your own receiver and transmitter from a kit, although these kits are not inexpensive. This kind of project is not recommended for beginners in radio, and should *not* be attempted until you have built less complicated gear. Anyhow, few new hams can bear to wait for months to get on the air until they have become skilled enough to build a complicated transmitter or receiver.

Rich, WA1UAW, and Lou, K1LK, began their ham careers with the purchase of a Heathkit HW101 transceiver from an experienced local ham who had built it himself from a commercially-available kit. After a few months of operating the Heathkit, which is an excellent transceiver, we decided to buy a new transceiver with more versatility and additional features such as RIT (receiver incremental tuning) which lets you change the frequency of the received signal by a few Hertz without changing your transmit frequency. The two of us studied the alluring advertisements in the ham magazines, read their advertising literature, talked to literally dozens of hams at the local ham club and on the air, and finally decided on the transceiver which, after five years of hard use, is still giving faithful service. This set is the Kenwood TS 520, a popular rig which was manufactured in Japan, and although now superseded by several model changes which have improved operation and operating convenience, is still in fine condition.

ANTENNAS

High power will certainly improve your chances of making radio contacts when atmospheric conditions are poor, but it is a fact that doubling transmitting power will not double the strength of the radio signal. Surprisingly enough, the increase in signal strength due to increasing TX power, although noticeable, is much less than one would expect. For this reason, hams with limited budgets invest in good antenna systems instead of in high powered amplifiers to increase signal strength. It is a truism that a dollar spent on the antenna has a higher payoff than a dollar spent on an amplifier. Antennas designed for Novice operation are inexpensive and easy to put up in most locations, although good indoor antennas for apartment dwellers may be difficult to design. The same antenna is usually used for receiving and transmitting. The antennas which are most popular with Novices are the half-wave dipole, the quarter-wave vertical and the "random-length" wire.

The dipole is probably the best antenna per dollar spent, but it requires a much greater area than other antennas. The dipole (two poles) is made of two copper or copper-clad steel wires of equal length which are trimmed as closely as possible to a length which is one quarter of the wavelength on which you intend to operate. The dipole will be resonant, that is, it will carry the maximum current and emit the strongest signal, if it is cut to just the right length for the operating frequency. One end of each wire is connected to a special kind of cable called a coaxial cable which runs down to the transceiver. Other types of connectors from the dipole to the transceiver are also used.

If you plan to operate on 3.725 MHz, a typical Novice frequency, the total length of the dipole may be calculated from a simple formula:

$$L = \frac{468}{F}$$

L is the length of the antenna in feet, and F is the frequency. For a frequency of 3.725 MHz,

$$L = \frac{468}{3.725}$$

which is equal to 125.6 feet. Each half or leg of the dipole is 62.8 feet which is one quarter of a wavelength. The total length of the antenna, not including the length of the rope or supports holding it up in the air, is 125.6 feet. You can see that you will need more than 45 yards to erect a dipole as it should be set up—in a long straight line and at least fifty feet in the air at each end. Although it is not quite as effective, the two antenna legs or "poles" may be arranged at an angle to each other as long as that angle is greater than 90 degrees. The center of such an antenna is usually higher than the ends. This "inverted vee" antenna is much like the one Louise and Charlie used. Rich, WA1UAW, and Lou, K1LK, also use the "inverted vee" because it takes up so little room. Since the dipole antenna is inexpensive and easily put up, it is the preferred Novice antenna, and it will get you on the air in the shortest time.

The vertical antenna is often used by amateurs who don't have enough room for the "inverted vee." The vertical is omni-directional. That is, it brings in signals and interference from all directions, and transmits in all directions. It must also be well grounded with

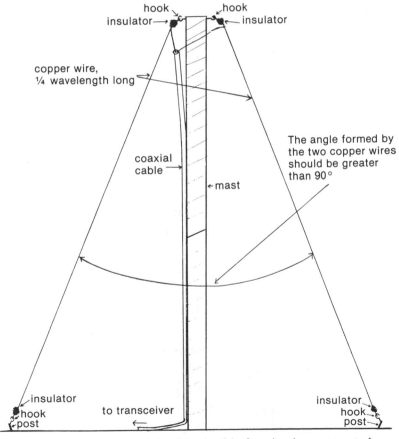

The thickness of the coaxial cables in this drawing is exaggerated, as compared to the thickness of the mast. (Illustration of inverted Vee antenna, drawn by WA1UAW.)

a network of wires running out from the base of the vertical mast which act as the other half of a dipole. Commercially manufactured verticals which take a minimum of room and need only a reasonable number of "radials" (the wires at their base) can be used on all novice frequencies and are relatively inexpensive and efficient.

The third type of antenna, the "random-length' antenna, is just a length of wire, usually copper or copper-plated steel, which is made as long as possible. This may have to serve as your antenna if you live in an apartment. The wire is usually attached to the walls or ceiling, and is run through several rooms to gain the greatest length. Unfortunately, since this kind of antenna is too short to "match" the transmitter properly, it will not be resonant, and as a result, the standing wave ratio (SWR) will be much too high. A high SWR may cause arcing (sparks jumping from power tubes to metal in the transmitter) and to early tube burnout. A high SWR means that too much power from the transmitter is being reflected from the antenna back into the transmitter instead of being radiated into space.

Since the length of the antenna cannot easily be increased, a device called an antenna tuner or transmatch is often used to "load" the antenna electronically. In a sense, the transmatch adds more length to the antenna so that the transmitter "sees" a resonant antenna and the reflected waves, although still present, are unable to re-enter the transmitter. Of course, the too-short "random length" antenna is still not resonant, and the antenna and transmitter are not properly matched. However, as long as the reflected waves are kept out of the transmitter, the SWR at the transmitter will be too low to cause damage.

An inexpensive instrument called a SWR bridge is

usually used to make SWR readings on a scale of 1 to 5. An SWR reading of 1 is ideal, but readings of 2 or less are satisfactory. The transmatch or antenna tuner is very useful whenever the match between the antenna and transmitter is poor. With it, you can use reasonably high power, but an inferior antenna will rarely give the signal quality of a properly matched antenna.

The new all solid-state transmitters are noticeably sensitive to an SWR which would not harm the older tube-type sets. Most solid state transmitters feature built-in devices which automatically reduce transmitter power whenever the SWR in the line from the antenna is higher than 2. When the SWR is much above 2, transmitter power may be so low that the transmitter is, in effect, shut off.

Dipole antennas are generally cut out a foot longer than the formula predicts, and then about an inch at a time is carefully trimmed from each leg until the SWR is at its lowest point. The frequency when this length is found is the resonant frequency of the antenna.

Some hams object to transmatches or antenna tuners because they usually have to be adjusted whenever the transmitting frequency is changed. However, you will soon learn to make these changes very quickly. WA1UAW and K1LK use a transmatch on their "inverted vee" so that they can work the entire 40 and 80 meter bands (7.000-7.350MHz and 3.500-4.000MHz) even though the antenna is only resonant at 3.5145 MHz.

There is a fourth type of antenna which some Novices and many other hams use—the "Yagi" which Tom Sachs saw at Louise's house. A 40 meter "Yagi" is so large that it is rarely used, although the smaller 10, 15 and 20 meter versions have become the most popular DX antennas. They are broadly resonant on each of these bands, two of which, the 10 and 15 meter bands, have

Novice portions. The great advantage of the "Yagi" or beam antenna is that is is highly directional, and gives a much greater signal gain in the direction to which it is turned than in other directions. This means that many interfering signals are eliminated while one's own signal strength is much greater. The beam is turned with an electric rotator, similar to but more powerful than TV antenna rotators since it is much larger and heavier than a TV antenna.

Although monoband (one band) "Yagi's" are manufactured, most hams buy tribanders (resonant on 10, 15 and 20 meters) because they are less expensive and much easier to install than three individual beams are. But, of course, they are also less efficient than monobanders. Tribanders cost much more than dipoles and all-band verticals since they are more complicated, and the antenna must be mounted 40 feet or more up on a sturdy steel or aluminum tower. Many hams have raised their beams to as much as 100 feet. The rule is, the higher the antenna, the greater the signal strength. Despite their higher cost, ranging from a few hundred dollars to thousands of dollars, most hams rely on the "Yagi," either a monobander or the 10,15 and 20 meter tribander for DX.

The SCARAVAN, operated by the Southcentral Connecticut Amateur Radio Association at Field Day. Photo taken by Steven Baratz.

(Top Left) Joe Rudi, star of the Los Angeles Angels baseball team. He is WA6PVA. Courtesy of Bob Jensen.

(Top Right) Sherrie, WD4IXV, a YL. Courtesy of QST Magazine.

(Bottom) Katrina, WD8NXU, a YL. Courtesy of QST Magazine.

(Top)
OSCAR photo, courtesy of *Ham Radio Horizons*.

(Bottom)
OSCAR 7 contact from Johnson Space Center. The operator in the center is Owen K. Garriot, W5LFL, scientist-astronaut. Courtesy of QST Magazine.

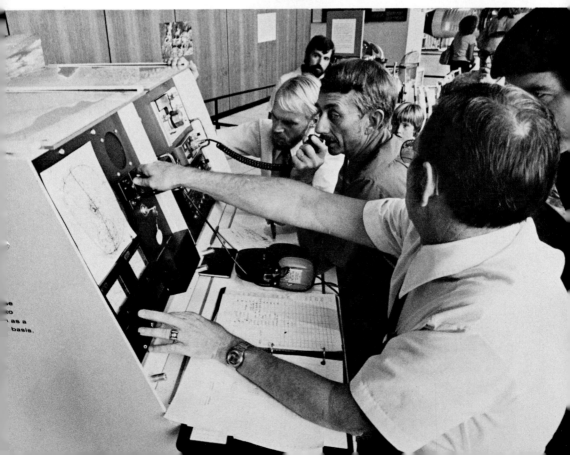

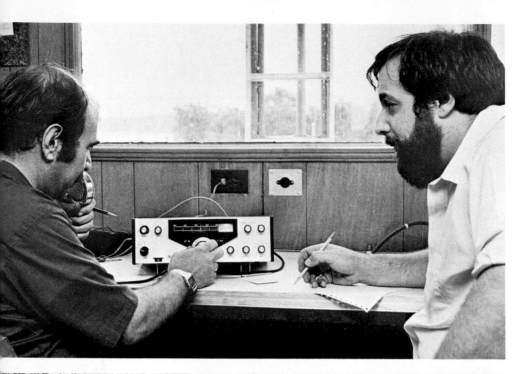

(Above) Rich, WA1UAW, operating in the shack. Photo taken by Steven Baratz.

(Top Left) George, WA1UBD, and Rick, WA1ZZO, operating in the SCARAVAN on Field Day. Photo taken by Steven Baratz.

(Bottom Left) XE1EPA, Gabriel, at a Mexican Field Day. Courtesy of QST Magazine.

(Above) K1LK's automobile license plate. Photo taken by Steven Baratz.

(Top) The Beam antenna used by Rich, WA1UAW, and Lou, K1LK. Photo taken by Steven Bratz.

Some of Rich's, WA1UAW, QSL cards.

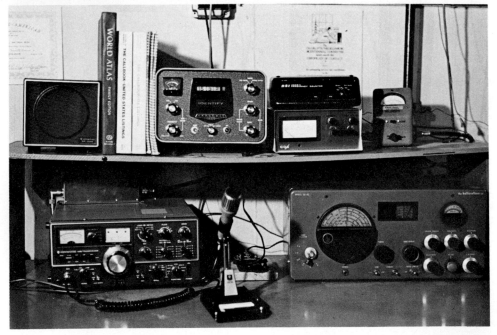

(Top) The transceiver used by Rich, WA1UAW, and Lou, K1LK. Photo taken by Steven Baratz.

(Bottom) The rig used by Rich, WA1UAW, and Lou, K1LK. Photo taken by Steven Baratz.

5 hunting DX

Many hams find that DX, the search for foreign ham stations, is the most fascinating part of ham radio. The DX "hound" tries to "work" (to contact) as many different countries and geographical zones as possible. These foreign contacts must be confirmed, and they are only confirmed when the DXer receives a QSL card from the DX station giving the date, time and frequency of the contact. For purposes of DX, many little-known islands and territories are counted as separate countries by the ARRL, even though they may be possessions of some country. Cocos Island, the Spratly Islands, Turks and Caicos Island and Juan de Nova, are examples of good, if not well-known, DX countries. Some prime DX countries are especially difficult to contact because no hams live there. Indeed, there may not even be any human inhabitants at all, and it is only when a group of hams arranges an expedition to one of these barren islands, carrying all their radio gear, electrical generators, food

51

and other necessities, that QSOs and QSL cards become available. News travels quickly when one of these rare DX locations goes on the air, and thousands of hams all over the world rush to their transmitters for those hard-to-get QSOs.

How thrilling it is for a DXer to talk, either on phone or CW, to far-off hams like 7Z2AP in Riyadh, Saudi Arabia, to FR7AI/J on Juan de Nova Island in the Indian Ocean, and to OX5BW, a scientist in Greenland, who is located just 500 miles south of the North Pole. They add to these thrills with awards which recognize their DX achievements. This recognition usually is in the form of special certificates and there are dozens of these awards open to qualified DXers wherever they live.

Most DXers, however, are not primarily motivated by these awards which they call "wall paper," or by the many DX contests which challenge them. What really spurs them on is the sheer fun of talking around the world to other hams. Successful DXing takes a combination of time, patience, good atmospheric conditions, and operating technique, and many thousands of hams have discovered that this branch of the hobby has become their special love. DXing is a way of traveling in a fraction of a second to far-distant places that, to visit in person, would take hours by airplane and weeks by boat.

VR6TC, Tom Christian, a direct descendant of the Mr. Christian of "Mutiny on the Bounty" fame, a mutiny which occurred on board a British warship in 1789, is the only ham on Pitcairn Island which lies thousands of miles from South America. Despite its remoteness, hams can bridge the many ocean miles to Pitcairn and to Tom Christian in the twinkling of an eye through the magic of ham radio. This is the kind of armchair adventure which is the real attraction for Dxers.

Nevertheless, awards are important to hams. As

soon as they have received QSL cards from 100 countries, worked either on CW or phone or both, they are eligible for the coveted DXCC (the DX Century or 100 club), sponsored by the ARRL. There are also DXCC awards for working 100 countries either on CW or phone, as well as for the much more difficult to attain goals of working 200 and 300 countries. One of the frustrations of the DX game is that many foreign hams, usually because they receive so many requests, send confirming QSLs months and even years late. This delay is made worse because of the length of time it takes for a card to come from an isolated outpost in the jungle or the desert where mail service is poor.

Despite these obstacles, or perhaps because of them, thousands of hams from all over the world qualify for DXCC every year. In addition to these awards and the others mentioned above, the ARRL and many other radio amateur organizations and publications such as *CQ* magazine sponsor such awards as WAZ (worked all geographic zones) and WPX (worked a certain number of different radio call prefixes). Hams who receive these eagerly-sought-after certificates are often commended in the radio amateur magazines. Everyone, with some patience and, of course, luck, can qualify for several awards. Even though the most famous DXers, such as W6AM and W8OZ have worked more than 350 countries, the Novice who confirms 100 countries or works all fifty states also makes his or her mark in the field.[1]

Needless to say, DXing, although enjoyable and exciting, requires a certain discipline of the operator and the application of proper operating procedures. In contrast to this discipline, American CBers obey few rules

---

[1]See "Some Call Prefixes From Around the World," Appendix p. 74-75.

of courtesy and operation. As a result, their frequencies are overcrowded, and usually unworkable. The widespread acceptance of good operating rules and of the need for self-discipline keeps the ham frequencies relatively free of unnecessary interference from the many hams using them.

The ham station which the writers of this book operate is a modest set-up by most ham standards. We run a Kenwood TS-520 transceiver feeding into a Mosley CL-33 three element beam antenna for 10, 15 and 20 meters perched on top of a 15 meter (50 foot) high tower. The power output of 80 watts is about one-tenth the legal amateur limit. Nevertheless, Rich, WA1UAW, has logged such rare DX as WR6TC, Tom Christian on Pitcairn Island, WE5BXQ/SU, a field mission in the Sinai Desert, JT1AN in Ulan Bator, Mongolia, north of central China and 9N1MM in Nepal. These exciting contacts were not made with high power or with an elaborate and expensive antenna system. They were made because WA1UAW first listened carefully on a number of frequencies before transmitting in order to find out the operating pattern of the DX station Rich wished to contact. Some DX stations indicate that they are ready for another contact by sending SK (the end of *this* QSO) or QRZ? (who is calling?), or even 73 (goodbye to the ham with whom they are talking). Once you recognize the pattern, you can decide on the best moment to call. Jim, 5Z4PP in Nairobi, Kenya, was snagged in just this way one Sunday afternoon. The bands are usually crowded on weekends as you would expect. That afternoon, more than a hundred amateurs called Jim when he came on the air. WA1UAW jumped in with the others at first, but his signal was lost in the massive interference of all these calls. Realizing his mistake, Rich stopped calling and listened intently to Jim's signal. He soon figured out the right moment to call. Jim seemed to be ready to talk to calling hams as soon as he signed a QSO with a 73, but the anxious crowd of hams on frequency was breaking in at the wrong time—calling just after Jim gave the station he was talking to a brief signal report, or when he had acknowledged another station. WA1UAW waited patiently until the other hams finished their poorly timed calls; when he was certain that he would not interrupt a QSO in progress, and in the total silence right after Jim's 73, WA1UAW gave his call letters just twice, and was immediately rewarded with a QSO and the promise of a QSL card. *Listening carefully is the name of the game!*

When they are QSOing DX stations, especially hard-to-get stations such as ZD8, Ascension Island and 9H4, Gozo, DXers should adhere to the "CPQ" rule which is, be Courteous, be Precise, and be Quick. Be courteous because whenever DX stations are on, there are usually dozens of American and Canadian operators waiting impatiently for their chance. *Never* interrupt a DX QSO in progress, and never call a DX station which is listening to another station unless you have emergency information to pass on. Many DX stations avoid hams who call during their QSO's. Hams who are guilty of this kind of interference are called "lids." Be Precise because clarity and emphasis in your speech or code transmission decreases time lost in repeating words or phrases. Be Quick because there are usually other hams who want that DX QSO. Clarity, however, should never be sacrificed for speed. Internationally-understood abbreviations, which are especially useful in CW QSO's, save a great deal of time.

By following the advice of the "ARRL DX Operating Guide" and by adhering to the "CPQ" rule, you will get your share of good DX. Hams who follow these rules become experts DXers who make many more good contacts than "lids" do.

"Lids" not only cause interference, but often, if they make a contact in the midst of a "pile-up" of calling hams, begin to "ragchew"—that is, to start a long discussion with the DX station, perhaps about current events, recent trips, or even their home life. "Lids" are inconsiderate persons, and ham radio can do without them. Fortunately, they are not numerous, but they are found on every ham band.

Even when the "big guns," those ham stations which go after DX with the maximum legal power of 1000 watts input, and with arrays of antennas which must be seen to be believed, seem to be monopolizing all the DX, a ham operating with low power and a simple antenna can usually get through. He or she can get through, that is, providing that good operating procedures are followed and atmospheric conditions are normal.

As soon as you receive your Novice ticket and your station is operational, you too can participate in the fun of hunting far-off lands through radio. Good DX-ing!

6
how to get the most out of your station

Soon after he began to study for the Novice license with Louise, his "Elmer," Tom Sachs bought a good used transceiver from a local ham so that he could practice copying the daily code transmissions from W1AW. Louise and Charlie helped him set up an 80 meter dipole cut to the right length for the Novice band.

Twelve weeks after his first meeting with Louise, a memorable day, the mailman left that long-awaited envelope from the Federal Communications Commission. When Tom opened it, he discovered that he had passed his test and that his call was KA1XYZ. "Now, at last, I can operate on my own," he thought. He knew that everything was ready to go—his rig, the straight key and antenna had already been tested by Louise and Charlie. He knew that the SWR was low and that the station was safe to operate and would cause minimal television and radio interference to his neighbors.

Tom was nervous about going on the air by himself so he telephoned Louise to tell her the great news and to ask her to come over to watch, just in case. Fortunately, Louise was free at that time and was soon there. She welcomed him once again into the fraternity of hams, and then said, "OK, Tom, now go ahead. It's time for your first QSO as KA1XYZ."

Tom's hand shook so that he had to wait for a few moments before turning the transceiver on and "tuning up." You, like Tom, will most probably be *very* nervous about your first contact. You must remember to be calm. Relax! If you need a pep talk, call your "Elmer," as Tom did.

Tom's transceiver was one of the older vacuum-tube types which require a "warming-up" and a "tuning-up." "Tuning-up" is adjusting the controls of your rig to produce the proper current flow into the antenna at the desired frequency; this procedure must be managed quickly and in the proper sequence of steps in order to avoid damage to tubes and to other working parts. Before "tuning-up," Tom listened carefully to the 80 meter Novice band, quickly scanning the frequencies from 3.750 to 3.800 MHz for an "opening," a frequency which is not in use by other novices. "Ah, here's one at 3.725 MHz," Tom exclaimed. He quickly connected the transceiver into a "dummy load," which is a piece of high resistance equipment specially built to take the full power of the transceiver without radiating any of it over the air. Hams must always try to avoid interfering with other hams. If you "tune-up" when the transmitter is connected to the antenna, radio signals which may cause interference will be emitted. The "dummy load" eliminates this interference and consequently is a very useful addition to a ham shack.

As soon as the rig was tuned, Tom disconnected the "dummy load" and reconnected the dipole lead-in to the transceiver. Now, at last, he was ready for his first QSO! But, Louise reminded him to listen again before sending the first CQ. He heard the sharp didahs of what at first seemed to be a QSO in progress. As he listened carefully, he heard "CQ CQ CQ CQ CQ CQ CQ DE KA2X-YZ CQ CQ CQ CQ CQ CQ CQ DE KA2XYQ K" sent at about eight words a minute, a speed which he could copy fairly well. Here was his chance! KA2XYQ was asking any listening ham on frequency to call him. With a shaking hand that seemed to be all thumbs, Tom touched the key and, much more slowly, sent his reply: "KA2XYQ KA2XYQ KA2XYQ DE KA1XYZ KA1XYZ KA1XYZ AR."

He stopped sending and waited anxiously for a reply. He shouted with joy when he heard "KA1XYZ DE KA2XYQ TNX FER UR CALL OM BT UR RST RST 579 579 BT QTH QTH PLAINBROOK NEW YORK PLAINBROOK NY JUST 30 MILES NORTH NEW YORK CITY BT NAME IS JIM JIM BT SO HW CPY? KA1XYZ DE KA2XYQ KN."

Even though Tom missed a few letters, he understood the whole message and quickly came back: "KA2X-YQ DE KA1XYZ R FB JIM BT UR MY FIRST CONTACT TNX VRY MUCH UR RST RST 599 599 BT QTH QTH BELLEVILLE NH BELLEVILLE NH NR LACONIA BT NAME TOM TOM BT HW CPY NW? KA2XYQ DE KA1XYZ KN."

The QSO continued for more than forty-five minutes as the two Novices exchanged information on their rigs, antennas, ages, schools and, of course, the weather. Tom finished his end of the QSO with this message: KA2XYQ DE KA1XYZ R R FB JIM BT TNX FER GREAT QSO MY FIRST BT WL SEND QSL CARD TO ADDRESS U GAVE BT PSE QSL FOR MY FIRST QSL CARD BT ENJOYED QSO ES HPE CUAGN SN ES WL SAY 73 BT TNX AGN SK KA2XYQ DE KA1XYZ."

When Jim came back with his "final," he wished Tom a good day and told him that he would QSL right away. Tom turned to Louise who said, "Tom, I'm very proud of you. That was well done. You made a couple of minor errors on some of the words, and you ran some of them together so that Jim had a little difficulty several times trying to figure out what you said. All in all, however, it was a very fine first QSO. Now, if the frequency is open, try a CQ call of your own."

Tom had begun his career as a radio amateur.

The messages which Tom and Jim sent each other were full of the abbreviations which hams learn very quickly on CW because they save time and are universally understood. If you have any difficulty in translating what was said, refer to the "Common Abbreviations" in the Appendix, 77.

Tom, of course, had been thoroughly prepared for his first QSO by Louise because he had already worked a number of hams at her home station as she stood by. He knew and observed the rules for proper operating procedure which are:

1. Listen carefully on and near the frequency on which you wish to transmit.
2. Do *not* "tune-up" on the air! "Tune-up" with a "dummy-load," an inexpensive piece of equipment.
3. After "tuning-up," listen again.
4. Don't interrupt a QSO (unless there is an emergency) until the operators sign off, or sign with the symbol "K" which means that others are invited to join in.
5. Make your CQ calls short, with not more than five or six CQ's in a row, and with your call sign given not more than three times. Continue to call CQ for one minute and no longer. This gives listeners a chance to get ready for the contact. This is a simple call:

"CQ CQ CQ CQ CQ DE KA1XYZ KA1XYZ KA1XYZ CQ CQ CQ CQ CQ CQ CQ DE KA1XYZ KA1XYZ KA1XYZ K." Then listen for a response. Note that endless CQ's will drive your listeners to other frequencies.

6. If you accidentally interrupt a QSO or a CQ call, apologize and look for a clear frequency. As a matter of courtesy, hams will send the Morse code letters "IE" or the abbreviation "QRL?" even if the frequency appears to be open. This is the courteous ham's way of asking, "Is this frequency clear?" If it is in use, one of the hams in the QSO will say so. Such courtesies are necessary because ham bands are often crowded. Only a "lid" "tunes up" mindlessly right on a working frequency and sends a long string of CQ's without first listening.

Amateurs are sometimes unaware that they are interfering with other amateurs, or that their transmitters are sending out "spurious" signals, signals on an unintended frequency, caused by improper adjustment of their transmitters. The American Radio Relay League has established a corps of volunteer "Official Observers" to monitor the ham bands for improper transmissions such as those described above. When the "OO," the "Official Observer," finds a violation, he or she sends the offending ham a note explaining the improper transmission. This is a "friendly" warning. However, the Federal Communications Commission also monitors the ham bands. If a violation is detected, the FCC will send the offender a "Citation." This "Citation" must be answered promptly with an explanation of why the violation occurred and how it has been corrected. Some of the most common violations are operating out of the authorized band, failure to identify properly, using excess power (Novices may not run more than 250 watts input to the final stage of their transmitters), and excessive interference to local radio and TV sets. Failure to make an appropriate correction can result in a fine, loss of license and even imprisonment in the most serious cases. This severe punishment is rarely necessary because many violations are unintentional and are easily remedied. Understanding of the FCC regulations and adhering to them will help you to have an enjoyable ham career.

Tom had been so thoroughly briefed on proper operation that he followed the rules without having to think about them. Because of this training, his many contacts were pleasurable for all concerned. Tom dreaded being called a "lid." He knew, that with the right procedures, *he* would never have that name applied to him.

However, he had also been drilled on an even more important aspect of good operation—the commandment of *SAFETY FIRST!* There are always risks with electrical equipment, especially radio equipment since the voltage inside a transmitter or receiver is high enough to cause severe electrical shock or even death. "RF," radio frequency radiation from an improperly adjusted transmitter or antenna, can cause skin burns. Therefore, *SAFETY FIRST!* must be the motto of every ham. The ARRL "Safety Code," given below, has been widely accepted. Post a copy of this code in your ham shack and work area:

1. KILL ALL POWER CIRCUITS COMPLETELY BEFORE TOUCHING ANYTHING BEHIND THE PANEL [of the transmitter] OR INSIDE THE CHASSIS OR THE ENCLOSURE [of the transmitter or transceiver].
2. NEVER ALLOW ANYONE ELSE TO SWITCH THE POWER ON AND OFF FOR YOU WHILE YOU'RE WORKING ON EQUIPMENT.
3. DON'T [test your equipment] WHEN YOU'RE TIRED OR SLEEPY.

4. NEVER ADJUST INTERNAL COMPONENTS BY HAND. USE SPECIAL CARE WHEN CHECKING ENERGIZED CIR-CUITS.

5. AVOID BODILY CONTACT WITH GROUNDED METAL . . . OR DAMP FLOORS WHEN WORKING ON THE TRANSMIT-TER.

6. NEVER WEAR HEADPHONES WHILE WORKING ON GEAR.

7. FOLLOW THE RULE OF KEEPING ONE HAND IN YOUR POCKET [this will help to keep electric current from passing through your body].

8. INSTRUCT MEMBERS OF YOUR HOUSEHOLD HOW TO TURN THE POWER OFF, AND HOW TO APPLY ARTI-FICIAL RESPIRATION.

9. IF YOU MUST CLIMB UP A TOWER TO ADJUST AN ANTENNA, USE A SAFETY HARNESS. NEVER WORK ALONE.

10. IF YOU MUST CLIMB A TREE, OR WORK ON A ROOF, REMEMBER THAT YOU'RE NOT STANDING ON THE GROUND. THAT FIRST STEP DOWN CAN BE A VERY LONG AND PAINFUL ONE. NEVER WORK ALONE.

11. DEVELOP YOUR OWN SAFETY TECHNIQUE. TAKE TIME TO BE CAREFUL. DEATH IS PERMANENT.

Although the following local "saying" is not one of these rules, it is also worth remembering: *NEVER FEAR ELECTRICITY, BUT YOU HAD BETTER DAMN WELL RESPECT IT*.

All hams must be safety minded even though the ARRL "Safety Code" applies primarily to hams who do their own equipment and antenna work. It is a very good idea for the new and inexperienced ham to ask an experienced ham to check his or her antenna and gear for safety, just as Louise and Charlie checked Tom's equipment.

One more precaution must be mentioned--to pro-tect against the awesome power of lightning. In some parts of the country, the great plains or on hilltops, antennas may be the highest objects in the region and make good targets for lightning. The old saying that "lightning never strikes twice" is completely untrue. Many radio amateurs can testify to the fact that *their* towers have been hit more than once.

It is very difficult, if not impossible, to protect against a direct lightning strike, or even a heavy concentration of static electricity which can produce enough current to cause damage. The *safe* course is to *DISCONNECT* all antennas and power lines in the shack before the lightning storm arrives. The disconnected antenna lead-ins should be connected to a good ground such as a *metal* water pipe (preferably copper or iron). Disconnect all power cords because lightning, striking a power line at some distance, can travel through the line into your home. As a matter of routine, each antenna and tower should also be grounded to minimize lightning damage, even though all inside power lines and antenna lead-ins are disconnected. The chances are that nothing will happen to *your* home in a lightning storm, but one can never be too careful. The references in Chapter 7 will give you more information on lightning protection.

These safety precautions may seen to call for a lot of care to prevent accidents which will probably never take place. ACCIDENTS DO HAPPEN, HOWEVER, AND VERY OFTEN THEY HAPPEN TO PEOPLE WHO SHOULD KNOW BETTER! Safety rules are not difficult to apply, and following them will increase your enjoyment of radio operation, which is what ham radio is all about.

In short, amateurs who act courteously on the air and safely for themselves and their families will have a lifetime of pleasure in the wonderful world of ham radio.

7

where to get help

Tom Sachs, like many hams, had to start from the beginning because he knew so little about electrical and radio theory. Although the Novice examination is not difficult to pass because the theory and practice you need to know is elementary (remember—a kindergartner passed this test), some study is required. If you work with an "Elmer" as Tom did, he or she will expect you to do some studying on your own. When you meet with your "Elmer," you will want to be ready to discuss the questions on which you will be tested. Don't waste your time and your "Elmer's" time by expecting the work to be done by your teacher—after all, you will have to pass the examination by yourself. In addition, you will have to practice sending and receiving the Morse code at home. Your "Elmer" will listen to your sending and will also send code at several different speeds to you; one session a week with your "Elmer" for an hour or so will

65

not increase your code speed enough. That's why practice at home is necessary.

If you attend local ham club classes, you will also be expected to come regularly and to be prepared. The volunteer teacher will probably lecture once a week to a class of from ten to thirty people, ranging in age from pre-teens to senior citizens. He or she will not be able to give much individual help, although there will be several times each period when your instructor will ask for questions, or if the topic under discussion is fully understood. The success rate for those who take the Novice or General test after regularly attending ham club classes is very high.

Some boys and girls, however, have passed their Novice test and even the General class examinations almost entirely through regular study and code practice, although they usually ask an experienced ham to help them make their first station operational. These boys and girls used some of the books which are described in the next section. Many of these books are available in public libraries, at the local ham club, or from nearby amateurs. It is a good idea to buy one or more since they are inexpensive paperbacks which will be good reference sources for years to come. They are stocked by many bookstores, by stores selling radio amateur equipment, and by mail from the publishers. Five of the most useful books are listed, together with a selected group of helpful articles taken mainly from *Ham Radio Horizons,* a magazine which is published for the new amateur. Many additional books and articles could be mentioned, but those listed below will be very helpful.

GOOD REFERENCES
FOR THE BEGINNING AMATEUR

1. Martin Schwartz, *Amateur Radio Theory Course,* Ameco Publishing Corp., 1979, paperback. This is a comprehensive book which will also help you prepare for the General and more advanced licenses. Certain sections are especially written for Novices. Practice questions similar to those on the FCC test are included.

2. *Tune in the World With Ham Radio,* American Radio Relay League, 2nd edition, paperback. This is the primary text to study for the Novice examination. It has been tested with thousands of beginners and is probably the most widely used introductory manual.

3. *The ARRL Novice Q and A Book,* American Radio Relay League, 1979, is a pocket-sized paperback in question and answer form. It gives a good review of the theory and practice discussed in references 1 and 2, and includes a sample FCC Novice test. It is possible, if you wish to do it, to memorize the answers, but that isn't the purpose of these books which is to bring out the important technical ideas simply and in a readily grasped form.

4. *The Radio Amateur's License Manual,* American Radio Relay League, 1980, paperback. This study guide for all license classes is more suitable for the advanced examinations than for the Novice test.

5. *Ameco 701 Questions and Answers Guide for the Novice Exam,* Ameco Publishing Corp., 1979. This paperback is more detailed than the *ARRL Novice Q and A Book,* and will be handy and serviceable.

67

USEFUL REFERENCES
IN THE HAM MAGAZINES

Antennas

JAMES R. FISK, "Dipole Antennas," *Ham Radio Horizons,* Jan., 1978, pp. 18-27.

DOUG DE MAW, "Antenna Accessories for the Beginner," *QST,* Feb., 1979, pp. 15-19.

Getting on the Air

KEN POWELL, "Getting on the Air: The Practical Approach," *Ham Radio Horizons,* Aug., 1978, pp. 50-54.

JIM BARTLETT, "Novice Questions and Their Answers," *QST,* May, 1979, pp. 34-36.

JAMES R. FISK, "Get on the Air on a Budget," *Ham Radio Horizons,* March, 1977, pp. 62-73.

CARL T. THURBER, "Designing Your Amateur Station," *Ham Radio Horizons,* Aug., 1978, pp. 44-49.

Lightning Protection and Safety

CARL T. THURBER, "Lightning and the Ham Shack," *Ham Radio Horizons,* July, 1978, pp. 22-27.

JAMES R. FISK, "Fire Prevention in the Ham Shack," *Ham Radio Horizons,* April, 1978, pp. 24-32.

Mastering the Code

CLAY LASTER, "A Plan for Morse Code," *Ham Radio Horizons, May, 1977, pp. 20-25.*

ALFRED WILSON, "Some Ideas for Learning the Code," *Ham Radio Horizons,* Jan, 1978, pp. 32-35.

GEORGE HART, "Learning Code by Osmosis," *QST,* Aug., 1979, pp. 58-59.

Operating Your Station

THOMAS F. MCMULLEN, "Amateur Radio Adventures for You and Me," *Ham Radio Horizons,* April, 1979, pp. 34-41.

JANICE SHILLINGTON, "Some Advice for Beginners," *Ham Radio Horizons,* Oct., 1977, 42-44.

68

ABELARTO J. MASSA, "How to Be a Lid," *Ham Radio Horizons, Sept., 1978, pp. 46-49.*

WILLIAM VISSERS, "Tune Up Swiftyly, Silently and Safely," *QST,* Dec., 1979, pp. 42-43.

LEE AURICK, "Things Your Elmer Forgot to Tell You," *QST,* Nov., 1979, pp. 62-63.

BOB LOEHER, "The Far-Horizon—An Evening of DX," *Ham Radio Horizons,* March, 1977, pp. 46-53.

JOSEPH J. CARR, "Some Cures for High SWR," *Ham Radio Horizons,* June, 1978, pp. 20-23.

CARL T. THURBER, "Matching Your Way to DX: A Look at the Transmatch," *CQ,* Feb., 1980, pp. 11-21.

OSCAR

ANTHONY R. CURTIS, "Riding High With OSCAR Satellites," *Ham Radio Horizons, March, 1977, pp. 18-23.*

Public Service

BRIAN E. PETERS, "Public Service Before Disaster Strikes," *QST,* April, 1979, pp. 52-53.

MICHELLE BARTLETT, "Rehab Radio," *QST,* Sept., 1979, p. 60.

COURTNEY HALL, "Rescue of a Castaway," *Ham Radio Horizons,* Jan., 1979, pp. 54-61.

Repeaters

GERALD R. PATTON, "Introduction to Repeaters," *Ham Radio Horizons,* Sept., 1977, pp. 12-23.

Amateur Radio Magazines

The important magazines for amateurs are *QST, Ham Radio Horizons, 73, CQ, Ham Radio and World-radio.* All are published monthly. Popular electronics magazines also contain materials of interest to radio amateurs, but the six listed above are written specifically for hams.

QST is the official magazine of the American Radio Relay League. Membership in the League includes a subscription to this magazine which publishes articles of technical and general interest, together with DX reports and news items about its members. Two of its special attractions are the many commercial ham equipment ads, and the "Ham-ads" section in which hams advertise equipment which they wish to sell or are looking for.

Ham Radio Horizons is published by the same company which publishes *Ham Radio*. Since it is written for the beginning amateur, you may find it to be the most helpful magazine. As you have already noticed, most of the references in the *"Useful References in the Ham Magazines"* section of this chapter are taken from it. Together with *QST, Ham Radio Horizons* will give you the latest information on developments of interest to the Novice. *Ham Radio,* its sister magazine, is probably too technical for the beginner.

73 is a large, sprightly, irreverent publication which carries a wide range of articles for amateurs, including computer applications. It has, as one would expect, a very large circulation. *73* is well-known for its many equipment ads which amateurs study eagerly as they plan for new gear to upgrade their shacks.

CQ magazine, one of the oldest in the field, is respected for its strength in reporting DX news and for its construction articles. It is well worth reading.

Worldradio is somewhat different from the other magazines in that it is more of a newspaper which features news items of interest to hams. It also publishes columns on "Public Relations," the "American Radio Relay League," amateur radio in aviation, "DX World,"

"Repeaters," "Maritime Mobile" and "AMSAT OSCAR." Construction articles and many commercial equipment advertisements add to its value.

Addresses of Amateur Radio Magazines

QST, American Radio Relay League,
225 Main St.,
Newington, CT 06111.

Ham Radio Horizons and *Ham Radio*,
Greenville, NH 03048

CQ,
76 North Broadway,
Hicksville, NY 11801

73,
Peterborough, NH 03458

Worldradio,
2120 28th St.,
Sacramento, CA 95818

appendix

THE MEANING OF CALL LETTERS

All amateur calls have three parts. The first part tells what country the call is assigned to. The second part gives the region of the country, and the third part identifies the person who has that call. For example, the "WA" in WA1UAW tells listening amateurs that they are listening to a ham station in the United States. The "1" tells them that it is in New England, and the "UAW" is for Rich. K5XZ is also American since "K" also designates the United States, the "5" locates it in the southwest, and "XZ" specifies the individual.

DISTRICTS AND REPRESENTATIVE CALLS IN THE UNITED STATES

District 1: The states of Connecticut, Maine, Massachusetts, New Hampshire, Rhode Island, and Vermont. Typical calls are WA1UAW, K1LK, KA1XYZ, N1XZ, and AC1X.

73

District 2: New Jersey, New York. W2CXM, K2AA, KB2ABC, and AA2XZ.

District 3: Delaware, Maryland, Pennsylvania, District of Columbia. W3RQ, K3RT, WA3LQZ, KA3NXB, and N3NX.

District 4: Alabama, Florida, Georgia, Kentucky, North Carolina, South Carolina, Tennessee, and Virginia. WB4BED, K4MB, KA4CDU, N4XZ and AC4B.

District 5: Arkansas, Louisiana, Mississippi, New Mexico, Oklahoma, and Texas. W5FQD, K5AR, KA5FQQ, WB5LLY.

District 6: California. W6LM, WA6RRP, K6ND, N6XZ, AC6B.

District 7: Arizona, Idaho, Montana, Nevada, Oregon, Utah, Washington, Wyoming. W7DR, WA7ANV, K7YLE, N7XA.

District 8: Michigan, Ohio, and West Virginia. W8NQ, W8NQR, K8AD, KA8BD.

District 9: Illinois, Indiana, and Wisconsin: W9QA, K9DE, W9BBT, N9AR, KA9DDN.

District 10: Colorado, Iowa, Kansas, Minnesota, Missouri, Nebraska, North Dakota, and South Dakota. WA0YYA, W0AZ, K0AF, WB0ADR, N0XD, N0ABD.

The states of Hawaii and Alaska are given special calls as are the territories and other United States possessions. Some typical calls for these regions are:

Hawaii: KH6NO, KH6GPO, AH6B, AH6FG, KH6AD, KH6ART
Alaska: KL7CW, LK7JHI, AL7C, AL7BD, WL7R
Puerto Rico: KP4AA, KP4AGE, NP4R, WP4CD
Midway Island: KM6FC, AH6F, AH6DE
Virgin Islands: KV4BY, KP4B, KP4RT
Wake Island: KW6HD, AH6N, KH6DR

SOME CALL PREFIXES FROM AROUND THE WORLD

The United States AA-AZ, N, K, W
Australia VH-VN

Burma XZ
Chile CE
Czechoslovakia GK, GL
France F
Greenland OX
Hong Kong VS6
Italy I
Kuwait 9K
United Kingdom G
Mexico XA-XI
USSR U
Israel 4X
Canada VA-VG

THE STORY OF
CALL SIGNS

Radio amateurs made their appearance in the United
States soon after Marconi sent the first radio message
across the Atlantic Ocean in 1901. Their numbers grew
rapidly since there were no government laws regulating
the use of the airwaves and many amateurs made up
their own calls. In 1913, licensing regulations were
passed by Congress. In less than a year, more than 2000
amateur licenses were issued. By 1914, more than 5000
licensed amateurs were active and there is good reason
to believe that at least that many more were operating
without licenses. The designations of W, A, K and N for
the United States had not yet come into being, so stations were given such calls as 2MN, 6PZ and 1AW. As the
number of hams increased, it became necessary to add a
third letter for the new hams, and calls like 1AAW, 3AFV
and 6ZAC came into use.

In 1927, the Federal Radio Commission was created to control all radio communication in this country. One of its first acts was to extend all existing radio amateur licenses until 1928 when the license period was limited to one year, renewable on request. In 1934, a new regulating authority, the Federal Communications Commission, took over the duties of regulating radio transmissions. At about this time, the present system of prefixes was adopted. With some changes to allow for the many new calls needed because of the increasing number of hams, this system has been in use now for nearly fifty years.

Some hams have kept the original calls issued to them before 1920. 1AW, originally Hiram Percy Maxim's call—he had been one of the founders of the ARRL—is now W1AW, the ARRL station in Newington, Connecticut. 1GC, Fred Brill's call in West Haven, Connecticut, is still Fred's call as W1GC. These calls which are more than fifty years old are treasured by the "old timers" in the hobby. "1 × 2" calls, such as W1VW and K1LK, usually indicate Extra Class, although many hams who never upgrade to the Extra Class still retain their precious "1 × 2's".

TYPICAL CALLS
FROM OTHER COUNTRIES

Bahrain: A9XAK, A9XX
Chile: CE1AE, CE3ACB
Azores Islands: CT2AC
Andorra: C31DL
Federal Republic of Germany: DB1FG, DF1SX, DJ3AY
Spain: EA1EJ, EA5HI

Guadeloupe and French St. Martin: FG7AB
Great Britain: G2AIH, G3CU, G8FPK
Japan: JA1BAJ, JH3YYB, JR4FK, JA0BCO
Argentina: LU1AAZ, LU2XA, LU5IB
Czechoslovakia: OK1AL, OK3TBM
Belgium: ON1AO, ON4MK
Sweden: SK2AN, SL0CG, SM5EGH
Poland: SP1FLP, SP4KI, SP9CHN
Costa Rica: TI2FB, TI3OJV
Gabon Republic: TR8AB, TR8SS
Soviet Union: UA1AV, UA6RD, RA3ADE, UQ2BP,
    UK5OAJ
Australia: VK1ZD, VK3ALQ, VK7AK
Hong Kong: VS6AZ
India: VU2ABR, VU2XW
Mexico: XE1ABD, XE2MVS
Indonesia: YB1AD, YD0LC

COMMON CW ABBREVIATIONS

ABT — About
AGN — Again
ANT — Antenna
B4 — Before
C — Yes
CNDX — Conditions
CFM — Confirm
CQ — An invitation for
        anyone to call
CU — See you
CUAGN — See you again
CUD — Could
CUL — See you later
DE — From
DX — Foreign stations
ES — And

FB — Fire business
FER — For
FREQ — Frequency
GB — Goodbye
GN — Good night
GE — Good evening
GND — Ground
GUD — Good
HI — Laughter
HPE — Hope
HR — Here
HV — Have, High voltage
IE — Is the frequency busy?
N — No
NG — No good
OM — Old man
OB — Old boy
OT — Old timer
PSE — Please
PWR — Power
QSL — Confirm contact with
a QSL card
R — Roger, Received
RST — Signal report of *r*eadability,
*s*trength, *t*one quality
RX — Receiver
SASE — Self-addressed
stamped envelope
SIG — Signal
SRI — Sorry
SSB — Single Side Band
TNX — Thanks
TX — Transmitter
UR — Your
VY — Very
WUD — Would
XMTR — Transmitter
XTAL — Crystal
XYL — Married lady
YL — Young lady

73 — Best wishes
88 — Love and Kisses

Q SIGNALS

Q signals are internationally understood abbreviations for certain kinds of information and questions. When sent without the question mark, they are statements. With the questions, they are requests for information. Only a few of the most common Q signals are given below:

QRA?	What is the name of your station?
QRL?	Are you busy? Is this frequency busy?
QRM	There is a lot of interference by other stations on your frequency.
QRN	There is a lot of static on your frequency.
QRP	I am transmitting with low power.
QRS?	Shall I send more slowly?
QRT?	Shall I stop sending?
QRX	Wait, I shall send again soon.
QRZ?	Who is calling me?
QSB	Your signals are fading.
QSL?	Will you acknowledge receipt of my transmission?
QSO	A two way contact
QSY	I shall move to another frequency
QTH	My location is . . .

PROCEDURAL SIGNS

Procedural signs are abbreviations which tell the listener what is to take place. Most are written with a bar over them to indicate that they are sent as one word without a break between the Morse code letters.

PROCEDURAL SIGNS

Procedural signs are abbreviations which tell the listener what is to take place. Most are written with a bar over them to indicate that they are sent as one word without a break between the Morse code letters.

Morse Code Characters	Abbreviation	Meaning
—•• •	DE	This is
•—•—•	AR	The end of a transmission when replying to a CQ
—•—	K	Please call—this is the end of the transmission
—•——•	KN	Only the station I was talking to should reply
•—•	R	All of your message heard
—•••—	BT	Universal punctuation mark for a pause
••• —•—	SK	I'm finished with this call, but will take others.
—•—• •—••	CL	I'm closing the station now.

THE HAM RADIO MORSE CODE

• Dih   – Dah

Letters		Numbers	Punctuation
A •–	N –•	0 –––––	comma ––••––
B –•••	O –––	1 •––––	period •–•–•–
C –•–•	P •––•	2 ••–––	question mark ••––••
D –••	Q ––•–	3 •••––	pause (BT) –•••–
E •	R •–•	4 ••••–	
F ••–•	S •••	5 •••••	
G ––•	T –	6 –••••	
H ••••	U ••–	7 ––•••	
I ••	V •••–	8 –––••	
J •–––	W •––	9 ––––•	
K –•–	X –••–	10 •––––	
L •–••	Y –•––	11 •–––– •––––	
M ––	Z ––••	20 ••––– –––––	
		45 ••••– •••••	

FCC AMATEUR RADIO STUDY GUIDE*

The FCC regularly revises the study guides on which the amateur license tests are based, and the study guide presented below is the latest revision. The Novice class test is based on the FCC's "Element 2 Syllabus" or study guide which has nine sections.

These sections are:

1. Rules and Regulations
2. Electrical Principles
3. Signals and Emissions
4. Circuit Components
5. Practical Circuits
6. Operating Procedures
7. Antennas and Feedlines
8. Radio Wave Propagation
9. Amateur Radio Practice

---

*The quoted materal and the "Study Guide for the Amateur Radio Operator License Examinations" is taken from PR Bulletin 1035, Jan. 1980, Federal Communications Commission, as published in the March, 1980 issue of *QST*, pp. 55-56.

FCC GUIDELINES FOR
THE NOVICE EXAM

The study guide given below "lists the rules, practices, procedures and technical material" with which you should be familiar before taking the Novice test. On first glance, it seems to be rather difficult, but as you read it carefully, you will realize that you already know several parts of these nine sections from the reading you have done in this book. The more technical parts are clearly and effectively presented in the manuals listed in "Good References for the Beginning Amateur," p. 000. Your "Elmer" or ham club teacher will also help you master these somewhat more demanding subjects.

The Novice license examination of 20 multiple-choice questions includes at least one question from each of the nine sections, with an emphasis on "Rules and Regulations," "Operating Procedures," and "Amateur Radio Practice." Since FCC tests are not available for study, we have prepared a "sample" Novice test similar to the FCC test, but with only 12 instead of 20 questions. Why not take this test now to see how many questions you can answer correctly? All that you need to know to answer questions 1,2,3,4,7,9 and 10 is in this book. But don't be misled! There is much more to learn. This book will give you a good start. Now the rest is up to you. Good luck!!

STUDY GUIDE FOR THE NOVICE CLASS AMATEUR RADIO OPERATOR LICENSE EXAMINATION

A. Rules and Regulations.

Define:
1) Amateur Radio Service
2) Amateur Radio operator
3) Amateur Radio station
4) Amateur Radio communications
5) Operator license
6) Station license
7) Control operator
8) Third-party traffic

Novice class operator privileges:
9) Authorized frequency bands
10) Authorized emission

Prohibited practices:
11) Unidentified communications
12) Intentional interference
13) False signals
14) Communication for hire

Basis and purpose of the Amateur Radio Service rules and regulations:
15) To recognize and enhance the value of the amateur Radio Service to the public as a voluntary, non-commercial communication service, particularly with respect to providing emergency communications.
16) To continue and extend the Amateur Radio operators' proven ability to contribute to the advancement of the radio art.

17) To encourage and improve the Amateur Radio Service by providing for advancing skills in both the communication and technical phases.
18) To expand the existing reservoir within the Amateur Radio Service of trained operators, technicians, and electronics experts.
19) To continue and extend the radio amateurs' unique ability to enhance international good will.

Operating rules:
20) U.S. Amateur Radio station call signs 2.302 and FCC Public Notice
21) Permissible points of communication
22) Station logbook, logging requirements
23) Station identification
24) Novice-band transmitter power limitation
25) Necessary procedure in response to an official notice of violation
26) Control operator requirements

B. Operating Procedures

1) R-S-T signal reporting system
2) Choice of telegraphy speed
3) Zero-beating received signal
4) Transmitter tune-up procedure
5) Use of common and internationally recognized telegraphy abbreviations, including: CQ, DE, K, SK, AR, 73, QRS, QRZ, QTH, QSL, QRM, QRN

C. Radio Wave Propagation

1) Sky wave; "skip"
2) Ground wave

D. Amateur Radio Practice

1) Measures to prevent use of Amateur Radio station equipment by unauthorized persons

Safety precautions:
2) Lightning protection of antenna system
3) Ground system
4) Antenna-installation safety procedures

Electromagnetic compatability—identify and suggest cure:
5) Overload of consumer electronic products by strong radio frequency fields
6) Interference to consumer electronic products caused by radiated harmonics

Interpretation of SWR readings as related to faults in antenna system:
7) Acceptable readings
8) Possible causes of unacceptable readings

E. Electrical Principles

Concepts:
1) Voltage
2) Alternating current, direct current
3) Conductor, insulator
4) Open circuit, short circuit
5) Energy, power
6) Frequency, wavelength
7) Radio frequency
8) Audio frequency

Electrical units:
9) Volt
10) Ampere

    11) Watt

    12) Hertz

    13) Metric prefixes: mega, kilo, centi, milli, micro, pico

F. Circuit Components

Physical appearance, applications, and schematic symbols of:

    1) Quartz crystals

    2) Meters (D'Arsonval movement)

    3) Vacuum tubes

    4) Fuses

G. Practical Circuits

Block diagrams:

    1) The stages in a simple telegraphy (A1) transmitter

    2) The stages in a simple receiver capable of telegraphy (A1) reception

    3) The functional layout of novice station equipment, including transmitter, receiver, antenna switching, antenna feedline, antenna, and telegraph key

H. Signals and emissions

    1) Emission type A1

Cause and cure:

    2) Backwave

    3) Key clicks

    4) Chirp

    5) Superimposed hum

    6) Undesirable harmonic emissions

    7) Spurious emissions

I. Antennas and Feedlines

*Necessary physical dimensions of these popu-
lar high-frequency antennas for resonance on
Amateur Radio frequencies:*
1) A half-wave dipole
2) A quarter-wave vertical

*Common types of feedlines used at Amateur
Radio stations:*
3) Coaxial cable
4) Parallel-conductor line

SAMPLE NOVICE TEST QUESTIONS

1. An amateur radio operator is a person who:
   a). has a pecuniary interest in amateur radio
   b). is interested in radio technique solely with a personal aim and has no interest in making money from amateur radio
   c). operates CB only
   d). has declared his or her interest in taking the Novice examination
   e). has any government radio license

2. It is good operating procedure to:
   a). listen on frequency before transmitting
   b). use maximum power for communication
   c). "tune-up" without a "dummy" load
   d). call CQ for at least five minutes at a time
   e). operate with a high SWR

3. All amateur radio stations must have:
   a). a transceiver
   b). a control operator

c). an amplifier

d). an SSB transmitter

e). a 40 meter antenna

4. Novices may not:

    a). send CW at more than 10 words per minute

    b). operate with more than 250 watts input to the final stage of their transmitters

    c). use a beam antenna

    d). operate at a frequency of 3.75 MHz

    e). use a transceiver

5. The Novice frequency of 3.75 MHz is the same as:

    a). 15.1   meters

    b). 10.3   meters

    c). 2.0   meters

    d). 7.35 meters

    e). 80.1   meters

6. The unit of potential difference is the:

    a). watt

    b). kilowatt

    c). ampere

    d). volt

    e). ohm

7. A megahertz is:

    a). 1000 hertz

    b). 1,000,000 hertz

    c). 1000 cycles per minute

    d). 1,000,000 ohms

    e). 10 farads

8. The unit of electrical inductance is the:

    a). farad

    b). henry

c). ohm
d). watt
e). ampere

9. A halfwave dipole cut for the 80 meter Novice
band is about:
a). 80 meters long
b). 80 feet long
c). 126 feet long
d). 252 feet long
e). 43 feet long

10. The purpose of an antenna tuner is to:
a). limit transmission power
b). increase SWR
c). keep the transmitter on frequency
d). match the transmitter to the antenna
e). increase receiver sensitivity

11. This is the electronic symbol for a:
a). vacuum tube
b). resistor
c). diode
d). transistor
e). tetrode

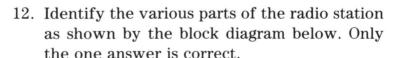

12. Identify the various parts of the radio station
as shown by the block diagram below. Only
the one answer is correct.

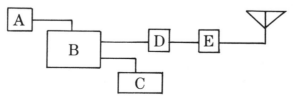

a). A is the low pass filter   d). D is the antenna
b). B is the transceiver   e). E is the key
c). C is a low-pass filter

Correct Answers
to the Novice Test Questions

1. b).	7. b).
2. a).	8. b).
3. b).	9. c).
4. b).	10. d).
5. e).	11. d).
6. d).	12. b).

index

Louis Kuslan is a graduate of the University of Connecticut, and holds a M.A. degree and Ph.D. from Yale University. Dr. Kuslan is presently a professor of chemistry at Southern Connecticut State College, and his son Richard is a freshman at Cornell University where he is studying Chinese. Both father and son became interested in amateur radio when Richard was a student at Hopkins Grammer School in New Haven which had a ham radio club. Richard obtained his amateur radio license at the age of thirteen; he now holds a General Class license and is active in the ham radio club at Cornell. Dr. Kuslan has maintained his interest in this fascinating hobby and holds an Extra Class license. His call number is K1LK.